# The Official Small Business Guide to Marketing 2.0

# The Official Small Business Guide to Marketing 2.0

Internet Marketing Tactics that Will Help You Cut Advertising
Costs, Grow Profits & Crush Your Competition

## Jonathan Taylor

Printed in the United States of America

ISBN: 978-0-557-07710-6

# Contents

# Contents

# Introduction

We live in times of uncertainty, but also great opportunity. Uncertainty looms with much volatility in the markets and unemployment soars to the highest level in more than twenty years. I speak with a lot of business owners and most have the "batten down the hatches" approach to this recession—waiting and hoping it will blow over soon. They're afraid to spend much more on marketing and advertising, so they don't want to do anything. This is one approach for sure, but I think it's the wrong one.

There are a lot of reasons for how we got here, but I'm not an economist. As a marketing consultant, I want to focus on how small businesses should be responding to the changes ahead. Change is happening on a number of fronts, not just economic. Old forms of mass communication are dying. Old forms of marketing and advertising are dying.

Change is never comfortable. It's much easier to continue with what you have been doing for years. That's what newspapers did and look at where they are today. One by one, they're fading away. Our nature as human beings is to avoid change. It's uncomfortable. Finally, when we're forced into it, we complain, "I remember when things used to be a lot simpler."

Complaining is so much easier than getting innovative and changing with the times. Then there's the approach of sticking your head in the sand. You can also pretend that things like television commercials, newspaper ads, and mass mailings are still a good way to promote your products and services. If you long for the old days, you're in trouble. But, if you're a maverick that can see opportunities through newer forms of marketing—blog sites, social media, online PR, and podcasting—the future can be very bright. Some people would call me an optimist, you know, one of those glass-half-full type people. These types of people tend to annoy the doom and gloom naysayers.

But when else could an innovative small business owner armed with only a small flip camera, a laptop, and an Internet connection beat out the larger, stronger competition? How is this possible? Haven't you read the story of David and Goliath in the Bible? Goliath the larger, mightier warrior was struck down by a small Israelite named David; not by standing toe to toe with the giant, but by using his God-given skill with a sling. Your job as a small business owner is to master the skill of today's sling—online marketing. You don't have to compete on the same level with the bigger companies. You only have to outsmart them.

That's what I want to share in this book. You see, a fundamental change has happened over the last twenty years. Barriers have crumbled. Barriers that once kept the small guy from getting his message heard are now gone. Today, anyone who is creative and savvy enough can get noticed. In the age of online media, almost anyone who is truly remarkable at what they do (what author Seth Godin calls being a *Purple Cow*) [1] can build a loyal following. A writer no longer needs to wait to see if a publisher wants their book. They can start a free blog, build a loyal following, and when they are ready to self publish, they have a list of readers lined up and waiting for the first copies to come off the printing press.

I started out my sales career years ago with a company selling industrial equipment—specifically resin and fiberglass application technology. Getting out and meeting new customers and solving their problems was something I enjoyed. Along the way, I began to learn what selling was really all about. I had good advice from a sales manager who encouraged me to be a consultant, not just another sales person. I also began reading tons of books on marketing and sales. I was a voracious reader, and always hungry for new ideas to apply to my business. One incredible book that I came across (and it's still one of my favorites) was a book called *The Obvious Expert* by Elsom Eldridge.[2]

Eldridge talks about the importance of positioning yourself as an expert within your industry so that instead of chasing after business, you have people chasing after you. I learned that my task was to become a consultant, an authority within my field, not a salesman.

My number one job was to solve technical problems for customers. I realized that if I became an expert at this, my job would get a lot easier. No longer would I be just another sales guy, but a recognized expert. Along the way, I began to learn new ways of marketing and promoting myself. I realized that success takes more than just knowing a lot about your industry. You have to promote that knowledge and expertise as well.

In this book, I want to share some important strategies I've learned about online marketing.

At the end is a transcript from an interview I did with David Dutton, author of the book *Internet Empires.*[3] David is well-known as the *most connected man on the Internet.* He will share some of his own insight from the world of online marketing.

I hope you find that this book is not only a resource of ideas, but also an inspiration to start your own online marketing campaign. I hope you'll see that you too can use social media and e-mail marketing to promote your expertise. I must tell you up front, though, success won't come from implementing just one of these strategies, but rather a number of them at one time.

## Newspapers Are a Dying Breed

I'm not a stock analyst, but I have enough foresight to know it would be a huge mistake to buy stock in newspapers right now. The industry is going down faster than the *Titanic* and technology is the enormous iceberg that's sending it into the abyss. Since 2007, technology journalist Paul Gillin has been chronicling the print media's demise at NewspaperDeathwatch.com. The problem with newspapers is its inability to change with the times. Readers can easily access news from multiple sources these days, mostly online, and it's free. Anyone with an iPod or Blackberry can pull up the latest news with the touch of a button.

Why would anyone care about news that was written the day before? Newspapers are pretty stale compared to 24-hour cable news coverage and sites like Drudge Report that are updated every few minutes. In addition, there are millions of blog sites that provide their own perspectives of the latest happenings. The newspaper's classified ad revenue is shrinking with the onset of sites like Craigslist.com.

It's been predicted that more than half of the 1,439 daily newspapers in the U.S. won't exist by the end of the next decade. That's a significant decline over the next ten years.

Does it really make sense for businesses to sink money into print advertising any more?

## Throwing Money at Outdated Marketing

On February 1, 2009, I watched Super Bowl Forty-Three featuring the Pittsburgh Steelers and the Arizona Cardinals. It was an epic game that went back and forth until finally the Steelers sealed the victory with a touchdown pass from Ben Roethlisberger to Santonio Holmes with thirty-five seconds left in the game, much to my disappointment.

What didn't disappoint me was the story behind one of the commercials played during the Super Bowl. It was a Doritos commercial created by two unemployed brothers from Batesville, Indiana. Their low-budget production won the annual Super Bowl Ad Meter Contest, beating out advertising giants like Anheuser

Busch and Coca-Cola. Let's get this straight; two guys without jobs come up with the best commercial during the biggest entertainment event of the year?

Here is what *USA Today's* Bruce Horovitz said about the rookie upset:

> For the first time, it wasn't an ad agency that created the best-liked Super Bowl commercial. It was two unemployed brothers from Batesville, Ind., whose ad for Doritos—created for an online contest for amateurs—won them $1 million from Doritos maker Frito-Lay, and leaves ad pros with a lot of 'splaining to do.[4]

Welcome to the new age of marketing, where a couple of guys and a cheap video camera can create more buzz than Madison Avenue. The Internet is breaking down the barriers of communication to the public. Business owners can now get their message out without spending a fortune.

Today's economic times are causing many companies to re-think how they spend their marketing and advertising dollars. This book will teach you, as a small business owner, to implement these new strategies of Marketing and PR. Most cost little to nothing. The new tactical weapons of promotion include:

- Autoresponders
- Blogging
- Content Rich Sites
- Online PR
- Podcasting
- Video Marketing
- Social Media
- Relationship Marketing (Offline Greeting Cards)

I will walk you through each one of these in this book. The

point of teaching you all of these is to get you implementing them all at once. Don't count on just one alone. Implement or find someone to implement all of these if possible.

**Using New Marketing Media**

Let's use the real-estate industry as a good example for new types of marketing media. Goodness knows they need to implement new technologies during times like this. Here's the problem—almost all realtors are doing the same thing. They hand you a business card with the name of their company and Web site. Some actually do have their own Web site, but it's usually just another portal for doing the same thing their company's site does—showing photos of houses for sale.

What if, however, you ran across that one exceptional realtor? You know, the one that has his own online YouTube channel that features weekly "Tips for First Time Home Buyers." The one that also has a weekly show on BlogTalkRadio where he or she discusses buying and selling strategies during tough economic times. The one that has a Web site offering a free special report (Ten inexpensive strategies for improving your home's value) just for signing up for their weekly newsletter and updates. You'd start to notice that this realtor is doing something completely different from most. This person has branded themselves as a qualified expert, not just a salesperson looking to pull in the next commission.

New marketing is not about using one single online tool. It's about using a combination of web technologies that will promote your business virally. It's about using permission marketing to connect with your existing customers. As author Seth Godin describes it, permission marketing is the privilege (not the right) of delivering anticipated personal and relevant messages to people who actually want to get them.[5] It's about creating a written or video blog that educates your customers about your industry. It's about an online radio show. How relevant are social networking sites to your business?

Your job as a small business owner is to use these new forms of marketing to propel your business to greater levels of success.

## Branding Is the Name of the Game

Recently, I discovered a major leak in my roof during a three day torrential downpour. I located the primary source—the main ridge vent. My curiosity was sparked, so I jumped on the web, went to YouTube and looked up "leaky ridge vents." My search produced a number of videos done by one professional roofer, videos about what to look for when inspecting your roof.

I spent more than thirty minutes just watching these videos because they were so informative. At the end of each video, the roofer's Web site address would appear, letting people know where they could find him if they needed a free estimate. This one simple strategy on his part separated him from so many other competitors. He did something remarkably different. From these videos, you got the feeling that this person was a real expert, not some fly-by-night operation.

Small business owner Ben Argov writes a blog on wine storage. You can find it at wine-storage.blogspot.com. Ben educates the public on the importance of wine storage and also reviews wine cellars and cabinets. Ben's blog is not only a way to get new qualified buyers, but also a way of branding himself as the authority when it comes to wine cabinets.

My friend David Dutton, an Internet marketing consultant, has a great line that I love to use, "People root for underdogs, but they do business with experts." Let that sink in. People do business with authorities in their field. I'm willing to pay a little more money if I feel I am buying from a true expert.

I've been on the e-mail list of a local cigar shop for the past three years. I subscribe because I appreciate getting e-mails from them every now and then about the latest cigar dinners they are hosting, or the newest import ales they have just gotten in. The owner is a true cigar aficionado. I appreciate someone who really has a passion for what they do, and I'm certainly willing to buy from them, because I know I'm getting incredible value.

No matter what your business is about, product or service, for-profit or non-profit, you have the opportunity to promote yourself as a recognized expert.

## It's about Relationships, Too

People buy not only from experts, but companies they feel comfortable with—companies they recognize. If you asked the average advertiser how many times it takes an ad to run before there's a response, they'll say on average about seven times. First encounters rarely sell high-ticket items. Ads have to be seen over and over before something clicks. Relationships are similar. Sure, there's impulse buying, just like "love at first sight," but enduring relationships that create customers for life take time to build.

So why is it that permission-based e-mail marketing is still missing from so many businesses today? I see so many small business Web sites that neglect one of the most powerful aspects of marketing—relationship building. They have no way on their site of collecting their customer's e-mail address. What's the point of your site if you're letting people come and go without developing a long-term relationship? The purpose of your Web site is to build a list. I will go into the details of using permission marketing to market to your list further in chapter 2.

Social media isn't just for teenagers anymore. It's becoming an ever important tool in the world of business. Sites like LinkedIn, Facebook, and Twitter allow you to stay in touch with your customer base. By keeping them informed of the latest updates about your company, you give them the sense that they are a vital part of your organization. A number of companies are already using the power of social media to build relationships with consumers.

Blendtech has created their "Will it Blend?" videos demonstrating their blenders pureeing everything from iPhones to digital camcorders. Talk about fascinating; and they've created an incredible amount of buzz on the web by posting these videos on sites like YouTube. This simple idea has led to a five-fold increase in business for them. Why? It's real. It connects with people, and those people then share it with others. We'll discuss more specific strate-gies for using social media sites for your business in Chapter 3.

# Chapter One

# Content Is King

Statistics show that the majority of people only stay thirty seconds at any given site before clicking away. If that's the case, then you've got to have something to entice them to stay longer. A site that tells people who you are and how long you've been in business is not going to keep people interested. Let me be clearer—it's just plain boring. In order to get prospects to stay, you have to provide good information that will keep them clicking from one link to another all through your site. Content is king, as they say in online marketing. You need to have articles or videos related to your industry that people can download.

This applies to any industry. For example, Barger and Sons, a local water and sewer services company in the Knoxville area, has a page on their Web site titled "learning center." If you click on the link you'll find a wealth of articles, white papers, and videos on everything you might need or want to know about septic tanks and grease traps. I'm sure that may not sound very interesting, but if you ever get a backed-up system, you'll want to know all about what's going on and how to prevent the problem next time.

A local wine store that I purchase from has a Web site that features an "Easy Wine Reference Section." The page has links to information like "wine tasting basics" and "wine and food pairing." These sections contain a few short articles, but imagine what they could do if they followed the example of Gary Vaynerchuck's Wine Library TV (tv.winelibrary.com). They could have a video of the week on how to pair wine up with food, or a "wine tasting for dummies" for people who want to learn from the experts.

### Differentiate by Offering Good Information

Your web content should be customer focused. Find out what they are interested in. When analyzing your existing site, ask yourself the question, "Does it talk about our cutting edge, state of the art products and services or our commitment to total customer satisfaction?" Phrases like this have been so overused that they start to lose effectiveness over time.

Any real-estate agent can tell you on their Website how committed they are to getting your house sold. That should be a given. That doesn't impress me. What would impress me is a realtor who offers incredible value up front. They might have a mortgage calculator on their site to help me figure out monthly payments. They might have a page on their site that shows average real-estate prices in certain areas of their state. They might even have a free downloadable ebook on "The 7 secrets To Getting Your House Sold Quickly Even in a Down Market," or an audio report on "5 Simple Ways to Improve the Value of Your Home."

Their site might even have a link to a blog that features the latest news on the housing market. We'll talk about how to set up an effective blog in the next chapter. If they don't want to write out lengthy reports, they could use video or audio content for their site.

One realtor in San Diego does just that. With a pocket camcorder, Jim Klinge takes video of houses that are overpriced. He points out the flaws of each one, and explains why they aren't worth the asking price. In one video, he walks in and shows the inside of a house where the previous owners had stolen the decorative pillars off the wall. He laughs, "They took the pillars!"

He posts these videos to his Web site (www.bubbleinfo.com), which gets about two thousand hits a day. This realtor is what Jay

Conrad Levinson, author of the book *Guerrilla Marketing*, calls a Guerrilla marketer. By posting this information to his blog site, he is positioning himself as an advocate for the buyer—a realtor who's looking out for people who've gotten ripped off in the past.

He's getting buyers when other realtors are getting out of the business. In 2007, he sold sixty houses. In 2008, he sold forty-one, which considering the area and the current economic climate, is quite good.

**Making Your Content Viral**

Jim Klinge's guerrilla tactic is just one example of how content can spread. Videos can be picked up and shared with others all over the web. His videos are uploaded to YouTube and then posted on his site. People can view them and share them by visiting his YouTube channel and clicking the "share" link. His video can then be shared with others on MySpace, Facebook, or Twitter. Not only that, the video code can be picked up by others and embedded on other Web sites, making it viral.

Create content that's useful and spreads. You can post articles on free online directories like EzineArticles.com and Goarticles.com. These sites allow you to write articles on topics related to your field of expertise. At the end of each article, you can post a link in the signature box that directs people back to your site. Here is a list of the top twenty article directories according to Mark Mason at Masonworld.com. This site updates the list on a regular basis:

- Ezinearticles.com
- Buzzle
- SearchWarp
- GO Articles
- Article Alley
- Article Dash Board
- Web Pro News

- Article Click
- Amazines
- Article Nexus
- Idea Marketers
- Articles Sphere
- Articles Factory
- Article-Buzz
- Article Depot
- Article Garden
- Article Snatch
- Article City
- Upublish

Links to some of these sites can be found on the resource page in the back of the book. There are also article submitter software programs that allow you to submit your articles to a number of article directories at one time. One that's very popular among Internet marketers can be found at www.articlesubmitterpro.com. You might even want to hire it out using a virtual assistant.

If you offer written reports or ebooks on your site, you want to make sure you insert links through this information that directs people back to your services and products. Obviously, you're giving away free information, but *you* want that information leading them to the ultimate solution to their problems—you!

The information you provide on your site should be focused on educating and bringing value, but don't forget that your job is to position yourself as the primary solution to your customer's needs. Explain to them how you'll solve their greatest problem. A great example of this is the carpet cleaner whose report describes all the creepy parasites that get trapped in your carpet. I can see this carpet cleaner having a site where he posts videos of some of the most disgusting-looking carpet that he's had to clean.

## Using Online PR

If you have newsworthy content on your site, you can

utilize online PR sites like PRweb.com and PRnewswire.com. I'm reminded of the guys who gained national attention by showing off the chemical effect of dropping Mentos candy into a bottle of Diet Coke. Their videos spread like wildfire across the web, getting them picked up by news outlets, and finally a spot on the David Letterman Show.

News outlets are always eager for exciting content that may be timely or unique. You'll need to submit a press release in order to get picked up. Here are a few guidelines for writing an effective press release:

- Make it newsworthy. Don't try to promote a product or service directly. If it sounds like an advertisement for your product or service, it probably won't get picked up.
- Use a captivating headline that gets attention.
- Use illustrations of how your product has helped solve a problem. Give a real life story (not an advertisement).
- Relate it to current events. One of the biggest news items right now is the economy. What is your company doing to help others reduce costs during slow economic times?
- Make it unique. If you're launching a new product or service, you'll need some unique spin on it. There are plenty of new product launches going on all the time. What's different about yours? Think about Jim the realtor. He's doing something different.

One successful news release can generate tens of thousands of visitors to your site in one day. You certainly want to be prepared for the traffic you start getting. This leads us right in to our next section.

Chapter Two

# E-mail Marketing

One of the most under-utilized tools in marketing today with most small businesses is direct response by e-mail, or what Seth Godin terms in his book *Permission Marketing*. As I mentioned previously, permission marketing is offering useful content that people want. This can be accomplished through frequent e-mail updates, such as weekly news, tips, or even  specials that your company might be running.

I recently visited a local tire and service center to get my vehicle inspected. I could tell just from talking to the manager that business was down. Yet, when I went to pay for the service, they never asked for my e-mail address to send out sales promotions. I would have been happy to give it to them, but they apparently didn't see the value. Talk about wasted chances! It was a missed opportunity to put my information into a database so that they could send out e-mail coupons for oil changes, tire rotations, or tune-ups.

I thought that maybe the employee that I paid just forgot to ask, so I checked their Web site. There was no opt-in box where I could sign up for an e-newsletter. What I found was nothing more than what I like to call a "brochure site"—a site that tells you "Who We Are," "How Long We've Been in Business," and "How You Can Contact Us."

Sadly, this is still the format that so many small businesses are using for their Web sites. They allow IT guys or friends who know nothing about direct marketing to create their Web site. Very big mistake. It's money flushed down the drain every day. Instead, I would imagine some of them are paying hundreds of dollars to advertise in the local newspaper.

Similarly, the new wine store near my house has no way of opting in to an e-mail system either. It's a little better than the first example. They offer some information on their Web site on selecting the right wines, but how many busy people are going to take the time to visit their Web site? My guess is very few existing customers. Sure, they might have a few people visit their site who are looking for a wine store in the area. They'll stumble across the site to see the latest sales. But this is like having a billboard located on a dirt road. Wasted money!

They could save the expenses of radio spots and increase their profits at the same time by simply having an e-mail autoresponder for sending out news and updates on their specials.

**Create an E-mail Marketing Campaign**

An e-mail marketing campaign is essential for getting current customers to buy from you over and over again. One of the best systems that I've found is AWeber. You can find them at www.aweber.com. AWeber is a powerful tool for e-mail marketing. For $19 a month, you can use their online service to host all of your e-mail lists and create newsletters, autoresponders, or RSS to e-mail. This online software allows you to create an opt-in box and then gives you the html code so that you can place it onto your existing Web site. It's really very simple. AWeber also has online screencast tutorials that will teach you everything you need to know.

The opt-in box can be placed within the template of your existing site or show up as a light box over the existing web page. This opt-in form can be customized to ask customers for more than just their name and e-mail address so that you can get other detailed information on them. AWeber also offers double opt-in, which means that customers who sign up for your e-mail updates will have to confirm that they have indeed requested to be put on your e-mail list campaign. A confirmation link is sent to their e-mail address immediately after they sign up at your Website. This feature saves you from being accused of spamming.

Once you start getting sign-ups it's important to send them something of value. You don't want to bombard your customers with promotions. This is certainly the fastest way to kill the golden goose. Instead, provide them with a weekly newsletter offering tips or other information that will make them want to read your e-mails.

For example, the previously mentioned wine store has a section on their site called "wine reference" that includes information on wine tasting tips, wine terms, and wine and food pairing. This information could be re-purposed for a weekly newsletter. At the end of each newsletter they might place a special discount coupon that's only good for one week. This is not only a great way to bring customers in more frequently, but also a great way to educate them and provide something of value at the same time.

### Giving Something of Value

As I mentioned, in order to get people to sign up for your e-mail newsletter, you should offer them something of value. Simply offering to send them e-mail updates on your latest specials often times won't cut it. People get enough junk e-mail everyday, so the last thing they want is extra stuff to delete. That's why I recommend a "tip-of-the-week" e-mail—something that educates your customer. Also, you can offer a free report that they might find useful and informative. A free report could be something that you write (or have someone else write) that offers a solution or provides some education. Let me give you an example. I recently did some work with a property management company that rented cabins in the Smoky Mountains. They wanted to rent two of their larger cabins for corporate retreats. Their target market was small businesses that were interested in planning corporate retreats for their employees.

I suggested that they create a Website focused on their corporate retreat cabins and offer a special report entitled "Why Corporate Training Doesn't Work and What Your Company Can Do about It." The report was about fifteen pages and I had them pay a freelance writer to put it together. I then posted it on their Web site using an AWeber opt-in box. This report created enough interest from companies who were already coming to the site to find out about the corporate retreats. From this simple strategy, they were able to build a targeted e-mail list to which they could send updates, as well as special promotions.

**Power of One—Singleness of Purpose**

In order to get customers to sign up for your e-mail campaign, you really need to be focused on the objective. What I mean by that is letting them know what you want them to do as soon as they come to your site. If your opt-in box is hidden out of sight, or is crowded in with the other links on your navigation menu, then it's very likely most people won't even notice. Your objective is to make things clear. For many sites, having a squeeze page is the best way to go. A squeeze page is nothing more than a simple one page site that instructs the visitor what you want them to do, which, of course, is to sign up for your e-mail newsletter. After they sign up on the squeeze page, you can then have them directed to the main Web site that has all of the company info. Another option is to implement a light box on your existing site. A light box is like a pop-up ad, but far less annoying. The opt-in box simply fades in after you been on the site for a few seconds.

**Hiring Freelancers**

One of the biggest drawbacks in the minds of most small business owners to sending out e-newsletters is the time and effort it takes to put something like that together each week. They have little extra time as it is, so adding one more thing to think about each week isn't all that appealing. My suggestion is simple— outsource it. There are a number of ways to hire freelance writers who are skilled at putting together a newsletter. A few sites for finding qualified people are:

- www.elance.com
- www.guru.com
- www.rentacoder.com

You can also find virtual assistants who will sell blocks of their time each week for doing various tasks such as writing e-mails, letters, web design, and more. I've hired VA's in the past for about ten hours a week in order to get small jobs done quickly. If you need free reports to give away to your subscribers, you can hire a freelancer to do this also. I've used another Web site called www.need-an-article.net to hire writers for reports and articles. They charge about $5.50 for a 550-word article.

This is incredibly inexpensive for the quality of writing. Once you sign up as a member ($9.95 month), you can log in and send requests describing what type of article or report you need, and they'll usually have it back to you within twenty-four hours— sometimes sooner. I have a friend who used the writers on this site to build an entire travel Web site that ranks very high on Google right now.

**The Real Value in E-mail Marketing**

The biggest advantage to using direct response e-mail is that it gets your current customers buying from you again and again. The biggest mistake that most businesses make is wasting their advertising dollars on trying to get new customers. It takes twice as much effort to get a new prospect to buy from you than it does for a customer who's purchased from you in the past. It amazes me just how few small businesses realize this.

Restaurants are a great example. They have new patrons coming in every day. They could print a message on their receipts offering weekly coupons to customers who sign up at their Web site. Moe's Southwest Grill is a great example of this. If you visit their site, you can sign up for news, special promotions, and even a birthday gift. They realize that it's ultimately about keeping faithful customers coming back again and again. A number of restaurants are now following this strategy because it's easier and cheaper than advertising.

The real value is long-term relationships that will continue on for years if you communicate with them.

## Scientific Advertising as It Applies to E-mail Marketing

To illustrate the importance of advertising principles in your e-mail marketing, I've included four important sections taken from Claude Hopkins classic book *Scientific Advertising,*[7] written in 1923. The technology of how we deliver sales copy may change over time, but the principles of selling never do. Keep these in mind when you write, or hire someone to write, your own e-mail marketing campaign. My comments will be in brackets.

## Excerpts from *Scientific Advertising*

### Offer Service

Remember the people you address are selfish, as we all are. They care nothing about your interests or profit. They seek service for themselves. Ignoring this fact is a common mistake and a costly mistake in advertising. Ads say in effect, "Buy my brand. Give me the trade you give to others. Let me have the money." That is not a popular appeal. The best ads ask no one to buy. That is useless. Often they do not quote a price. They do not say that dealers handle the product. The ads are based entirely on service. They offer wanted information. They site advantages to users.

Perhaps they offer a sample, or to buy the first package, or to send something on approval, so the customer may prove the claims without any cost or risks. Some of these ads seem altruistic. But they are based on the knowledge of human nature. The writers know how people are led to buy. Here again is salesmanship. The good salesman does not merely cry a name. He doesn't say, "Buy my article. " He pictures the customers side of his service until the natural result is to buy.

A brush maker has some 2,000 canvassers who sells brushes from house to house. He is enormously successful in a line which would seem very difficult. And it would be for his men if they asked the housewives to buy. But they don't. They go to the door and say, "I was sent here to give you a brush. I have samples here and I want you to take your choice." The housewife is all smiles and attention. In picking out one brush she sees several she wants. She is also anxious to reciprocate the gift. So the salesman gets an order.

Another concern sells coffee, etc., by wagons in some 500 cities. The man drops in with a half-pound of coffee and says, "Accept this package and try it. I'll come back in a few days to ask how you liked it. " Even when he comes back he doesn't ask for an order. He explains that he wants the women to have a fine kitchen utensil. It isn't free, but if she likes the coffee he will credit five cents on each pound she buys until she has paid for the article. Always some service. The maker of the electric sewing machine motor found advertising difficult. So, on good advice, he ceased soliciting a purchase. He offered to send to any home, through any dealer, a motor for one weeks' use. With it would come a man to show how to operate it. "Let us help you for a week without cost or obligation," said the ad. Such an offer was resistless, and about nine in ten of the trials led to sales.

So in many, many lines. Cigar makers send out boxes to anyone and say, "Smoke ten, then keep them or return them, as you wish." Makers of books, typewriters, washing machines, kitchen cabinets, vacuum sweepers, etc., send out their products without any prepayment. They say, "Use them a week, then do as you wish. " Practically all merchandise sold by mail is sent subject to return. These are all common principles of salesmanship. The most ignorant peddler applies them.

Yet the salesman-in-print very often forgets them. He talks about his interest. He blazons a name, as though that was of importance. His phrase is, "Drive people to the stores," and that is his attitude in everything he says. People can be coaxed but not driven. Whatever they do they do to please themselves. Many fewer mistakes would be made in advertising if these facts were never forgotten.

[This is one of the biggest mistakes with e-mails today. They're filled with "we, we, we" instead of focusing on the customer's needs. Customers are always looking for solutions to their problems. Your e-mails should be crafted in such a way as to provide something they can use. If you want your customers to read your e-mails, don't start off by telling them how good your product or service is. Offer valuable tips, free downloadable reports, or gift certificates. ]

## Headlines

The  difference between advertising and personal salesmanship lies largely in personal contact. The salesman is there to demand attention. He cannot be ignored. The advertisement can be ignored. But the salesman wastes much of his time on prospects whom he can never hope to interest. He cannot pick them out. The advertisement is read only by interested people who, by their own volition, study what we have to say. The purpose of a headline is to pick out people you can interest. You wish to talk to someone in a crowd. So the first thing you say is, "Hey there, Bill Jones" to get the right person's attention. So it is in an advertisement. What you have will interest certain people only, and for certain reasons. You care only for those people. Then create a headline which will hail those people only. Perhaps a blind headline or some clever conceit will attract many times as many. But they may consist of mostly impossible subjects for what you have to offer. And the people you are after may never realize that the ad refers to something they may want.

[In crafting an e-mail marketing campaign, the purpose is always to get the reader's attention. Think, headline first. It's the first thing that people read when they glance at their inbox. You can be sure it will be the one thing that gets your e-mail either read or deleted. With marketing systems like AWeber.com, it's easy to give your headline that personalized touch by inserting your customer's name within the subject line. E-mail subject lines like "Hi Bill, here's the information that you might be looking for," can really capture their attention. ]

Headlines on ads are like headlines on news items. Nobody reads a whole newspaper. One is interested in financial news, one in political, one in society, one in cookery, one in sports, etc. There are whole pages in any newspaper which we may never scan at all. Yet other people might turn directly to those pages. We pick out what we wish to read by headlines, and we don't want those headlines misleading.

The writing of headlines is one of the greatest journalistic arts. They either conceal or reveal an interest. Suppose a newspaper article stated that a certain woman was the most beautiful in the city. That article would be of intense interest to that woman and her friends. But neither she nor her friends would ever read it if the headline was "Egyptian Psychology." So in advertising. It is commonly said that people do not read advertisements. That is silly, of course. We who spend millions in advertising and watch the returns marvel at the readers we get. Again and again we see 20 percent of all the readers of a newspaper cut out a certain coupon. But people do not read ads for amusement. They don't read ads which, at a glance, seem to offer nothing interesting. A double-page ad on women's dresses will not gain a glance from a man. Nor will a shaving cream ad from a woman.

Always bear these facts in mind. People are hurried. The average person worth cultivating has too much to read. They skip three-fourths of the reading matter which they pay to get. They are not going to read your business talk unless you make it worth their while and let the headline show it.

[Keep in mind that this was written in 1923. How much busier are people today? People won't take the time to read something unless it captures their interest right away. Your headline is what separates you from all the other junk solicitations. ]

People will not be bored in print. They may listen politely at a dinner table to boasts and personalities, life history, etc. But in print they choose their own companions, their own subjects. They want to be amused or benefited. They want economy, beauty, labor savings, good things to eat and wear.

[Your prospects are always tuned into that classic radio station WIIFM (What's In It For Me?), so make sure your copy speaks to their needs. ]

There may be products which interest them more than anything else in the magazine. But they will never know it unless the headline or picture tells them. The writer of this chapter spends far more time on headlines than on writing.

He often spends hours on a single headline. Often scores of headlines are discarded before the right one is selected. For the entire return from an ad depends on attracting the right sort of readers. The best of salesmanship has no chance whatever unless we get a hearing. The vast difference in headlines is shown by keyed returns which this book advocates. The identical ad run with various headlines differs tremendously in its returns. It is not uncommon for a change in headlines to multiply returns from five or ten times over. So we compare headlines until we know what sort of appeal pays best. That differs in every line, of course.

The writer has before him keyed returns on nearly two thousand headlines used on a single product. The story in these ads are nearly identical. But the returns vary enormously, due to the headlines. So with every keyed return in our record appears the headlines that we used. Thus we learn what type of headline has the most widespread appeal. The product has many uses. It fosters beauty. It prevents disease. It aides daintiness and cleanliness. We learn to exactness which quality most of our readers seek. This does not mean we neglect the others. One sort of appeal may bring half the returns of another, yet be important enough to be profitable. We overlook no field that pays. But we know what proportion of our ads should, in the headline, attract any certain class.

For this same reason we employ a vast variety of ads. If we are using twenty magazines we may use twenty separate ads. This because circulation's overlap, and because a considerable percentage of people are attracted by each of several forms of approach. We wish to reach them all. On a soap, for instance, the headline "Keep Clean" might attract a very small percentage. It is too commonplace. So might the headline, "No animal fat. " People may not care much about that. The headline, "It floats" might prove interesting.  But a headline referring to beauty or complexion might attract many times as many. An automobile ad might refer in the headline to a good universal joint. It might fall flat, because so few buyers think of universal joints. The same ad with a headline, "The Sportiest of Sport Bodies," might out pull the other fifty to one. This is enough to suggest the importance of headlines. Anyone who keys ads will be amazed at the difference. The appeals we like best will rarely prove best, because we do not know enough people to average up their desires. So we learn on each line by experiment.

But back of all lie fixed principles. You are presenting an ad to millions. Among them is a percentage, small or large, whom you hope to interest. Go after that percentage and try to strike the chord that responds. If you are advertising corsets, men and children don't interest you. If you are advertising cigars, you have no use for nonsmokers. Razors won't attract women, rouge will not interest men. Don't think that those millions will read your ads to find out if your product interests. They will decide at a glance— by your headline or your pictures. Address the people you seek, and them only.

[Just as in traditional sales copy, the best strategy in e-mail marketing is to always test different headlines to find out what pulls the best. Unlike sales letters, e-mail messages sent through software like AWeber can be analyzed soon after they are sent to see what the open rate percentage is.

To see a list of the 100 greatest headlines ever written, visit http://www.abraham.com/articles/100_Greatest_Headlines_ Ever Written. html. ]

## Being Specific

Platitudes and generalities roll off the human understanding like water from a duck. They leave no impression whatever. To say, "Best in the world," "Lowest price in existence," etc. are at best simply claiming the expected. But superlatives of that sort are usually damaging. They suggest looseness of expression, a tendency to exaggerate, a careless truth. They lead readers to discount all the statements that you make.

[Most people will automatically ignore claims that aren't backed up by specifics. You must quantify your claims. What makes this the best quality around? Exactly how much can you reduce your customers operating costs? Exactly how much time can you save them? Exactly how much in additional revenue can your product or service bring in?]

People recognize a certain license in selling talk as they do poetry. A man may say, "Supreme in quality" without seeming a liar, though one may know that the other brands are equally as good. One expects a salesman to put his best foot forward and excuses some exaggeration born of enthusiasm. But just for that reason general statements count for little. And a man inclined to superlatives must expect that his every statement will be taken with some caution. But a man who makes a specific claim is either telling the truth or a lie. People do not expect an advertiser to lie. They know that he can't lie in the best mediums. The growing respect in advertising has largely come through a growing regard for its truth. So a definite statement is usually accepted. Actual figures are not generally discounted. Specific facts, when stated, have their full weight and effect.

This is very important to consider in written or personal salesmanship. The weight of an argument may often be multiplied by making it specific. Say that a tungsten lamp gives more light than a carbon and you leave some doubt. Say it gives three and one-third times the light and people realize that you have made tests and comparisons.

A dealer may say, "Our prices have been reduced" without creating any marked impression. But when he says "Our prices have been reduced 25 percent" he gets the full value of his announcement.

A mail order advertiser sold women's clothing to people of the poorer classes. For years he used the slogan, "Lowest prices in America." His rivals all copied that. Then he guaranteed to undersell any other dealer. His rivals did likewise. Soon those claims became common to every advertiser in his line, and they became commonplace. Then under able advice, he changed his statement to "Our net profit is 3 percent." That was a definite statement and it proved very impressive. With their volume of business it was evident that their prices must be minimum. No one could be expected to do business on less than 3 percent. The next year their business made a sensational increase. At one time in the automobile business there was a general impression that profits were excessive. One well-advised advertiser came out with this statement, "Our profit is 9 percent. " Then he cited actual costs on the hidden costs of a $1,500 car. They amounted to $735, without including anything one could easily see. This advertiser made a great success along those lines at that time. Shaving soaps have long been advertised "Abundant lather," "Does not dry on the face," "Acts quickly," etc. One advertiser had as good a chance as the other to impress those claims. Then a new maker came into the field. It was a tremendously difficult field, for every customer had to be taken from someone else. He stated specific facts. He said, "Softens the beard in one minute. " "Maintains its creamy fullness for ten minutes on the face." "The final result of testing and comparing 130 formulas. "

Perhaps never in advertising has there been a quicker and greater success in an equally difficult field. Makers of safety razors have long advertised quick shaves. One maker advertised a 78-second shave. That was definite. It indicated actual tests. That man at once made a sensational advance in his sales. In the old days all beers were advertised as "Pure." The claim made no impression. The bigger the type used, the bigger the folly. After millions had been spent to impress a platitude, one brewer pictured a plate glass where beer was cooled in filtered air. He pictured a filter of white wood pulp through which every drop was cleared. He told how bottles were washed four times by machinery. How he went down 4,000 feet for pure water. How 1,018 experiments had been made to attain years to give beer that matchless flavor. And how all the yeast was forever made from that adopted mother cell.

All claims were such as any brewer might have made. They were mere essentials in ordinary brewing. But he was the first to tell the people about them, while others cried merely "pure beer. " He made the greatest success that was ever made in beer advertising. "Used the world over" is a very elastic claim. Then one advertiser said, "Used by the peoples of 52 nations," and many others followed.

One statement may take as much room as another, yet a definite statement may be many times as effective. The difference is vast. If a claim is worth making, make it in the most impressive way. All these effects must be studied. Salesmanship-in-print is very expensive. A salesman's loose talk matters little. But when you are talking to millions at enormous cost, the weight of your claims is important. No generality has any weight whatever. It is like saying "How do you do?" When you have no intention of inquiring about one's health. But specific claims when made in print are taken at their value.

[Sales letters filled with good emotional appeal often fail because they lack enough facts to justify the purchase. A good strategy in writing an effective letter is to start out mentioning the specific benefits a customer will receive and then build the case by introducing social proof. Using case studies and testimonials of satisfied clients is one of the most effective ways to offer compelling proof. ]

## Tell Your Full Story

Whatever claim you use to gain attention, the advertisement should tell a story reasonably complete. If you watch returns, you will find that certain claims appeal far more than others. But in usual lines a number of claims appeal to a large percentage. Then present those claims in every ad for their effect on that percentage. Some advertisers, for sake of brevity, present one claim at a time. Or they write a serial ad, continued in another issue. There is no greater folly. Those serials almost never connect.

When you once get a person's attention, then is the time to accomplish all you can ever hope with him. Bring all your good arguments to bear. Cover every phase of your subject. One fact appeals to some, one to another. Omit any one and a certain percentage will lose the fact which might convince.

People are not apt to read successive advertisements on any single line. No more than you read a news item twice, or a story. In one reading of an advertisement one decides for or against a proposition. And that operates against a second reading. So present to the reader, when once you get him, every important claim you have. The best advertisers do that. They learn their appealing claims by tests—by comparing results from various headlines. Gradually they accumulate a list of claims important enough to use. All those claims appear in every ad thereafter.

The advertisements seem monotonous to the men who read them all. A complete story is always the same. But one must consider that the average reader is only once a reader, probably. And what you fail to tell him in that ad is something he may never know. Some advertisers go so far as to never change their ads. Single mail order ads often run year after year without diminishing returns. So with some general ads. They are perfected ads, embodying in the best way known all that one has to say. Advertisers do not expect a second reading. Their constant returns come from getting new readers. In every ad consider only new customers. People using your product are not going to read your ads. They have already read and decided. You might advertise month after month to present users that the product they use is poison, and they would never know it. So never waste one line of your space to say something to present users, unless you can say it in your headlines. Bear in mind always that you can address an unconverted prospect.

Any reader of your ad is interested, else he would not be a reader. You are dealing with someone willing to listen. Then do your level best. That reader, if you lose him now, may never again be a reader. You are like a salesman in a busy mans office. He may have tried again and again to get entree. He may never be admitted again. This is his one chance to get action, and he must employ it to the full.

This brings up the question of brevity. The most common expression you hear about advertising is that people will not read much. Yet a vast amount of the best paying advertising shows that people do read much. Then they write for a book, perhaps—for added information. There is a fixed rule on this subject of brevity. One sentence may tell a complete story on a line like chewing gum. It may on an article like Cream of Wheat. But, whether long or short, an advertising story should be reasonably complete.

A certain man desired a personal car. He cared little about the price. He wanted a car to take pride in, else he felt he would never drive it. But, being a good business man, he wanted value for his money. His inclination was towards a Rolls-Royce. He also considered a Pierce-Arrow, a Locomobile and others. But these famous cars offered no information. Their advertisements were very short. Evidently the makers considered it undignified to argue comparative merits.

The Marmon, on the contrary, told a complete story. He read columns and books about it. So he bought a Marmon, and was never sorry. But he afterwards learned facts about another car at nearly three times the price which would have sold him the car had he known them. What folly it is to cry a name in a line like that, plus a few brief generalities. A car may be a lifetime invest-ment. It involves an important expenditure. A man interested enough to buy a car will read a volume about it if the volume is interesting. So with everything. You may be simply trying to change a woman from one breakfast food to another, one tooth paste, or one soap.

She is wedded to what she is using. Perhaps she has used it for years. You have a hard proposition. If you do not believe it, go to her in person and try to make the change. Not to merely buy a first package to please you, but to adopt your brand. A man who once does that at a womans' door won't argue for brief advertise-ments. He will never again say, "A sentence will do," or a name claim or a boast. Nor will the man who traces his results. Note that brief ads are never keyed. Note that every traced ad tells a complete story, though it takes columns to tell. Never be guided in any way by ads which are untraced. Never do anything because some uninformed advertiser considers that something right. Never be led in new paths by the blind. Apply to your advertising ordi-nary common sense. Take the opinion of nobody, whom know nothing about his returns.

[People are naturally attracted to a good story. We all love a good movie. Most of us love to hear someone else tell a great story. Have you ever heard someone say, "Let me tell you about the disaster that happened to me yesterday . . . " Naturally our ears perk up. We want to hear this dramatic story. The same is true with e-mails. I love to get e-mails from professional copyrighters because they typically begin with an intriguing story. Stories of people who have benefited from a product or service need to be used in your e-mail marketing. Don't bore your readers to sleep with endless facts. ]

Chapter Three

# Blogging for Business

There are more than 150,000 blogs created every day. Many are just a means for people to rant or communicate with friends and family, but blogs can be an effective marketing tool for a number of reasons. They are great way to build enormous trust with your customers.

A blog is an open forum that lets you communicate what's going on and, at the same time, lets your customers give feedback. It's also a way of building your reputation as the go-to expert in your industry. The more you write, the more attention you gain.

Let me give you a short example of the power of a blog in building your reputation as an expert.

Few people would have known who Jon Ostrower was just a few years ago. But that changed when he started blogging about the latest updates on the development of the Boeing 787. Ostrower had no aerospace training; neither did he have a back-ground in journalism. All he really had was a serious interest in what he was writing about. His readership, which started out at only 315, grew to well over 1.7 million. His status grew as well. His reputation as the inside man on the 787 landed him a job writing for trade journal *Flight International.*

**The Obvious Expert Blogger**

In his book The *Obvious Expert,*[8] Elsom Eldridge talks about the marketing power of being an author. Whatever subject you write on, you become the authority in that field. Eldridge is, of course, talking about self-publishing books, but I believe blogs are a great way to get started in building your professional reputation as well. More people are switching from printed publications to online news these days. Digital information is cheaper than paper and ink!

If you are a self-employed professional, you need a blog. If you own an insurance business, write about the changes within the industry or provide tips for saving money on car insurance. If you are a landscaper, write about landscaping tips. Remember the wine cabinet maker I mentioned earlier. I have a friend who works as a personal trainer. He wanted to create an online presence, so I suggested that he start with a blog that shares fitness and nutritional tips. He began posting and was surprised at how soon his clients were noticing

A blog presents you with a medium that your audience can access easily. If you post entries on a regular basis, include your blog address on any other printed materials you have such as business cards or brochures. If you post often enough and if your blogs are informative people might begin to subscribe so that they get automated updates every time you post.

I have a blog—jonathantaylorblog.com—that I've written posts on for the last two years. I try to post with regularity, although I occasionally fall behind. It's a great way of branding myself as a marketing expert and improving my writing skills at the same time. I find that the more I write, the better I get. Plus, a blog is free, so it costs nothing but my time to make posts 2-3 times a week.

**Turn Your Blog into a Book**

Many people like the idea of writing a book, but the thought of writing a 200-page book quickly begins to overwhelm them. Here's my suggestion—turn your blog into a book. As I write this book, I am using a free WordPress blog as a way to keep pages and chapters organized. This is beneficial for a couple reasons. I have my wife proofread it every day as I post new sections. She corrects any obvious errors before it goes through final editing. The other benefit is that, as I continue to write, I can build an online following.

Seth Godin, author of great books like *Permission Marketing* and *Purple Cow*, did this with one of his other books *Small is the New Big*. He took some of his most popular posts and compiled them into a 350-page book.

Julie Powell went from being unknown to a published author by creating a blog on her attempt to cook all 524 recipes from Julia Child's classic cookbook *Mastering the Art of French Cooking*. Her blog led to a publishing deal and a book, *Julie and Julia: 365 Days, 524 Recipes, 1 Tiny Kitchen Apartment*. This book sold 100,000 copies.

If you were to post just three times a week, at the end of one full year, you could have 156 pages completed. Or using the same strategy, you could have several small reports written each year for your business.

### Get Your Employees Involved

If you own a small business, you can have your employees blog. This might make some owners a little nervous, but it's a great way to create an open forum with your customer base. Obviously, guidelines will need to be set as to what they should be posting, but you do want them to be able to express ideas or solutions to customer complaints.

Back when I worked for an industrial equipment manufacturer as a sales rep, they allowed the sales force to post blogs discussing solutions to some of the biggest complaints we heard from our customers in the field. This was an innovative way for our company to address problems head on. We gathered feedback from plant managers and workers on problems they might be having and used it to write problem solving articles on our blog. On occasion, I even used the blog to provide testimonials from some of our satisfied customers. We were able to then direct them to the site so that they could post follow-up responses or additional questions from certain posts.

Blogging is simply a way of putting a face on your company. Your customers like to see some personality behind a name.

### Creating a Remarkable Blog

Anyone can get a free blog started using WordPress or Blogger. You can set an account up with either of these services and begin blogging in about five minutes. I recommend, however, having a blog uploaded onto your hosting account. This still costs nothing if you already have a host provider with your current site. The barrier to overcome is learning how to do it. You can pay someone to get it set up for you, but it's really not that complicated. I'll walk you through a few steps to getting started.

### Start with WordPress

I've used WordPress for about three years now. I started with a free version at www.wordpress.com and posted my articles on a regular basis. This was a big mistake, because after a year of getting used to it, I wanted to have a little more control over the settings. I ended up switching it over to another domain with the software loaded onto a web host provider. This made my traffic drop like a rock, since my new site wasn't indexed by search engines. You live and you learn.

Once you've secured a good domain name for a blog, you'll really want a host provider that makes it easy to install WordPress. There are two that I highly recommend because they have automatic installation with a few clicks. They are Bluehost.com or Hostgator.com. Either work great with WordPress and both have an application called Fantastico Deluxe that allows you to quickly install the WordPress software.

### Customizing Your Site

One of the best books I've found on customizing your

WordPress site is *WordPress for Dummies.* [9] Even if you outsource this part of the process, I'd recommend picking up a copy of this book just to get familiar with setting up an effective blog site. After you've installed the blog software, you'll notice that the theme of the site is rather basic. WordPress provides you with two default themes that aren't very impressive looking.

If you really want to add that personal brand to your site then you'll need to install a more attractive template. If you go to http://wordpress.org/extend/themes, you'll have a selection of more than six hundred themes to choose for your site. Once you've downloaded the theme you want, it's pretty simple to install. I usually install themes and other plugins using the main control panel in Hostgator. If you go to www.easywebsitetutorials.com, you can watch some video tutorials I've put together for installing a WordPress theme.

### Generating Traffic to Your Blog

Once you've created a customized blog, you'll want to make sure that you can generate traffic to it. The first priority is making sure that it shows up in the search engines. If there's one thing I've learned in Internet marketing, it's that search engine ranking is not an exact science. It can be tricky at times, because of the way search engines rank results.

Using keywords is a big part of generating traffic to your site. You'll need to find out what keywords people are searching for online that might be related to your business. There are a couple of free tools you can use to look for search volume. The first is Wordtracker (http://freekeywords.wordtracker.com). This version only measures search volume per day, but it's very informative when it comes to finding out what words and phrases people are using when they search for topics related to your niche. The other site that I use quite frequently is Google's free search tool (https://adwords.google.com/select/keywordtoolexternal).  The  Google tool measures searches by the month. By using these research tools, you can get a clear understanding of the demand for the subject you are using within the content of your site. Keywords need to be placed throughout the content of your blog post. There are also some useful tools in helping you optimize the title and description of your blog posts.

If you're using WordPress, which I recommend for anyone starting a blog, then you'll want to add some important plugins for optimizing your site. Plugins are software modules that help the main software application function better. If you use Mozilla Firefox as your Internet browser, you may have noticed that you can add these plugins to Firefox to make the browser more research friendly. Similarly, plugins for WordPress can be uploaded very easily onto the main site through the main control panel of your site. Two important plugins for optimizing your site are "All in One SEO" and Google (XML) sitemap generator. The "All in One SEO" plugin is simple to use. After you've installed it, you'll be able to set up each of the posts on your site with keyword tags. You can also use title posts and descriptions that are keyword specific.

The Google sitemap generator is an easy way of letting search engines know your web pages are ready to be crawled by little spiders (Spiders are software robots that gather information for search engine databases). You can find both of these plugins by going to http://wordpress.org/extend/plugins and doing a quick search for both of these. For a tutorial on how to install these plugins, visit http://easywebsitetutorials.com and you can find instructions under the "WordPress videos" page.

**Using Trackbacks for Traffic**

In addition to optimizing your site, there other ways of generating traffic. Think of the blogosphere as a large web of linked blogs. Trackbacks would be one set of those links. Using track-backs, you can link your blog post to another blogger's post and in the process get traffic from their readers.

For example, if you have a blog that discusses "car buying tips" and you find another blogger who writes a post on this particular subject, you can comment on his article by using the trackback feature. After you write a comment on your blog and send a trackback, the other blogger will be notified that you have commented on his article and a link back to your site will appear on his post. This is a way to increase your traffic coming from other sites. Don't use this feature, however, without offering something of worth to the previous author's piece. Otherwise, it will appear as nothing more than an attempt to spam.

A great way to find out if other bloggers are writing about your area of expertise is to set up a notice through "Google Alerts" (http://www.google.com/alerts). Just log in and enter the keyword you would like to be alerted to. Google will then e-mail you a listing of blog sites that are discussing that topic every day.

## Social Bookmarking

Another great way to get traffic to your blog is social book-marking. If you don't have a lot of experience with blogs or Web sites, you may not know what social bookmarking is or how it works. There are several social bookmarking sites such as Digg. com, StumbleUpon.com, Reddit.com, and others that are popular with the public. The sites are all arranged in categories by topic. This is where you will choose the right topic for what you are submitting.

When you sign up on one of the social bookmarking sites you will submit a title, keywords, a description of what you are submitting, and a url. The title should contain the primary keyword, as well as the description. The keywords you submit should be as relevant as possible. Make sure they are words in the content of what you are submitting. When people in the social network search for a specific item, your topic will have the greatest chance of being included in their search results.

People who write articles frequently for different Web sites use the social bookmarking sites to promote their content. This is how traffic is generated to your site, creating back links to your site as well. Members of the social bookmarking site can vote on your submission, which will allow it to move up the line to the number one spot. This is very important to the success of your site.

### How to Use Social Bookmarking

Before you submit your blog url to a social bookmarking site, you must register for an account. This is free and does not take long. After signing up for the account, you can log in and find the category that fits your blog site. Submit your site to the proper category. The more social bookmarking sites you are registered and submitted to, the more traffic you will receive.

You may want to do a search and find as many of the sites as you can. Make a list and start registering with each one. Keep

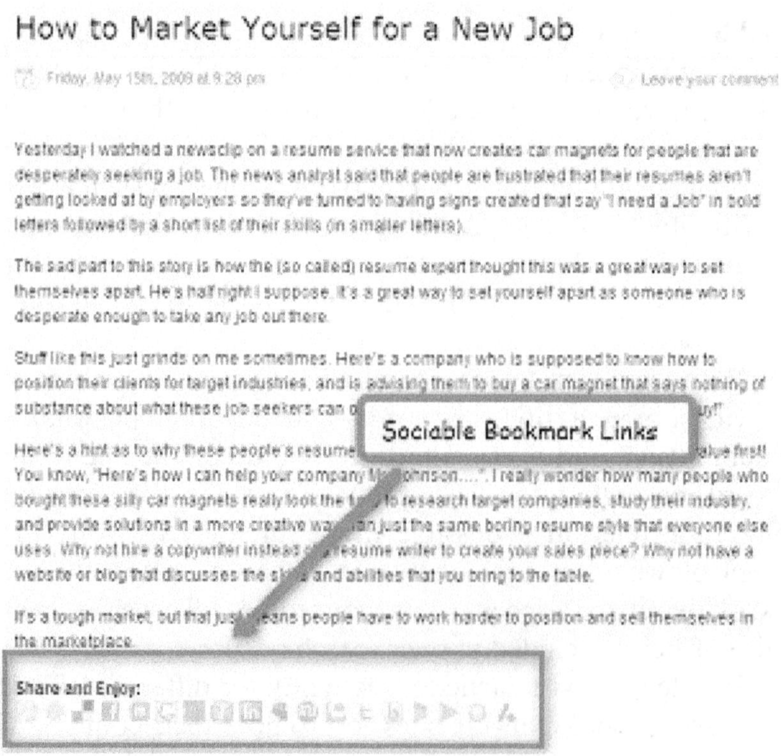

*Figure 1: Social Bookmarking*

a list of the ones you have registered with and your entire log in information. Depending upon your resources and time restraints, you may find that hiring an SEO company to submit your url to the social bookmarking sites is easier.

One of the best reasons for submitting your site to a social bookmarking site is the speed with which the site is indexed by search engines. Google, Yahoo, and other search engines will index the sites on social bookmarking faster than others. The quicker your site is indexed, the faster it will be listed on the search engines and generate traffic for you. As everyone well knows, being listed high in the search engines is the best way to generate traffic.

Another option is a service that automatically submits your content to many of the top social bookmarking sites. There are a couple of these around that you either pay a small fee of approximately three dollars a month or it is a free service, you just have to tolerate the advertisements. By using one of these services, one click will get your site submitted to many social bookmarking sites at once.

**Adding Bookmarking Plug-ins to Your Blog**

Another way to get your content spread using social bookmarks is to add a social bookmarking plug-in onto your blog so that at the bottom of every new blog post will be a social media button readers can click on to share an interesting article you've written.

This helps get your content spread virally throughout the web. The more people share your articles with others, the more traffic you get. You can find a number of different social bookmark plug-ins by simply googling the phrase "Social bookmark plug-in for Wordpress. "

# Chapter Four

# Marketing with Video

Video is growing at an incredible rate on the Internet. With so many video sharing sites these days, you're missing out on a valuable marketing tool if you're not creating content with a camcorder or screen-cast program. However, there's a right way and a wrong way to advertise with video. The worst possible way for your video to come across is as an advertisement. With so many videos out there, you have to really stand out by giving people a reason to watch your clip.

You've got to give them something interesting. If they sense that you're just trying to sell them something, they'll just click away, but if you're providing weekly how-to tips, then you're on the right track. As I mentioned previously, the roofer who had YouTube videos that showed what to look for when checking for leaks on your roof was giving out some good information.

A friend of mine who works as a personal trainer has his own show on a YouTube channel where he offers workout tips. He just recently bought a HD flip camera that he keeps in his pocket. In between sessions, when he gets the opportunity, he records short sessions on the go. The footage is far from spectacular. It's what I would coin a ghetto video, but it's good content and it's real to people. People would much rather see this than some boring, canned commercial.

Personally, I think we've only scratched the surface with video. We're now seeing sites like Hulu.com, where you can watch entire episodes of your favorite TV shows or older movies. It's really amazing and it offers some incredible opportunities for companies who want to advertise within those videos.

I recently purchased a .TV domain because I think that these domains will be the next dot coms, with more people creating video blogs. I'd recommend anyone grabbing a .TV domain for their personal name or their business name. You can use this site to create your own low-budget, yet creative commercial. I can't think of a better way to brand yourself as the expert if you are constantly producing helpful videos that add value to others.

For example, Bill Myers, a product developer, (www.bmyers. com) is constantly generating screencast videos on subjects related to producing and selling DVDs online. His site is a wealth of information. He markets his membership site by posting tons of videos on YouTube. These videos get viewed every day by hundreds of people. One of his videos comparing lavalier mics has generated more than seven thousand views.

**Getting Started with YouTube**

Setting up your own YouTube channel is relatively easy. You'll want to register if you don't have an account already. It takes only a few minutes. Make sure that you choose a username that brands your name to your business; a name that people will remember. For example, Gary Vaynerchuck of Wine TV has his own YouTube show and his username is WineLibraryTV, the same as his own Web site.

Once your account is set up, it's very easy to start posting video—just click "upload video. " For each video you upload, you can write a brief description and also include tags. Tags are needed so that people can find your site. So you'll need to use keywords that describe the content of your video.

Customizing your own channel is pretty straightforward too. Just click on "channel design" and you can set up your own color schemes, fonts, and background images. Now you're ready to start adding content.

Beside each new video you create is a url link that you can use to send people directly to your video, or you can copy the embed code just below that and add it to your own webpage or blog. I use the embed code feature to paste the code on a lot of my own Web sites. Recently, YouTube has added new features that allow you to customize the border and choose from different video sizes.

### Getting Subscribers

Just like a blog or a newsletter, you want people to sign up for

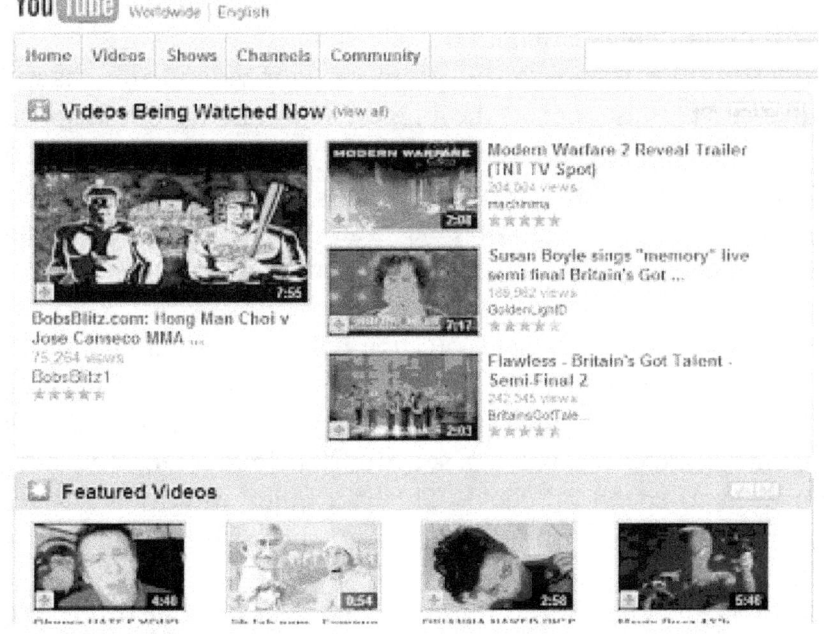

*Figure 2: YouTube Homepage*

all of your video updates. This is just another way to gain permission. Once people subscribe to your video channel, you've got a potential customer for as long as they continue to stay subscribed. One of the best ways to get subscribers is to begin subscribing to other video channels.

Try to focus on videos that have markets you want to attract. If you are an interior designer showcasing some of the recent homes that you've helped decorate, pick other channels that are relevant— real estate, home decorating, remodeling, etc. You also have the option of becoming a friend of someone, which in turn allows you to share videos privately. All the videos that you post will then show up on their channel. This can really boost your traffic.

To add someone as a friend, go to their profile page. There is a link entitled "Connect with (username)" that you'll want to click. Then you'll go to the "add as a friend" link.

**The Bottom Line Is Promotion**

YouTube allows you to promote your video to its massive audience. This is one of the biggest features at your disposal. You get a massive amount of traffic if your video is featured on YouTube's home page. Here's the kicker—there are only twelve slots available on the home page, and YouTube updates its site about twice a day. The likelihood that you'll get picked up at first is slim to none.

Another feature that YouTube has added is similar to Pay Per Click Advertising. You can decide where you would like your videos to appear and place bids for those category keywords. Just like Google adwords, you can set your daily budget for how much you want to spend on clicks. This is a quick way to get a large volume of traffic to your channel and then direct them to your site.

The most important thing to remember in all of this is to be promoting your primary business Web site. With all of the latest changes that YouTube has made, it's easier than ever. There is now a feature that allows you to add annotations within your video, so you can put the address of your main Web site within the video as a reminder for people to visit. You can also add a clickable link within the description box so that others can click straight to your site.

**Get Your Video to Spread**

There are a number of other video sites you'll want to utilize besides YouTube. A great tool that will help you upload video to all of them at once is called TubeMogel. You can find it at www.tubemogel.com. Just sign up for a free account and you can have your videos sent to YouTube and other similar sites such as Vimeo, Viddler, Yahoo, Metacafe, and others with just a few clicks. It's a simple way to direct traffic back to your site.

If you look at a lot of the top video marketers, they tend to post their videos at every possible sharing site online. If your video is really eye-catching or provocative, there's a chance that your video will be picked up and spread around the web. Your video could end up on Web sites you've never heard of. I suppose that's why they call it viral marketing.

Listed below are a few suggestions for getting your video to spread like wildfire:

- Be genuine—Don't be fake. People can see right through it if you have a canned speech. Relax and have fun with it. Some of the best videos are those in which people just shoot with nothing more than a cheap webcam.
- Be entertaining—Don't just talk about your business and what you do; give some real results. Think, "Will it Blend?" No sales talk is as effective as seeing that blender chop up an iPhone.
- Give Value—Give people a reason to spend their time watching your show. An auto repair shop could have a weekly shop segment where they discuss how to properly service your car or truck. If you're a remodeler, how about some video tips on laying ceramic tile?

Again you don't have to be fancy when it comes to production. The most popular YouTube video, "Evolution of Dance," was done with a low-budget camera, and it currently has over 115 million views. The desire to have the perfect video is what keeps many from doing video marketing. Don't worry about being perfect. Just grab a camera and start shooting.

Chapter Five

# Podcasting: The Value of Audio Content

Have you ever thought what it would be like to host your own radio show? Think of all the business you could get just from from being the go-to expert on the radio. You might not make it on the air the traditional way, but you can start your own radio show online and it only takes a few short minutes to get started. I'm talking about podcasting. Podcasting has been around for the last few years (it has slowed in popularity with the explosion of online video), but there are still a couple of outlets I would recommend for getting traffic and promoting your business. BlogTalkRadio.com and Podomatic.com are two that I want to discuss.

A podcast is simply a series of audio files that can be distributed online through webfeeds. These webfeeds can then send the podcasts to iTunes, allowing listeners to download the audio content onto their portable iPod. Through iTunes, listeners can subscribe to your podcast and these will be automatically down-loaded into their iTunes application each time you produce new content. My wife listens religiously to an online productivity show hosted by FlyLady each week via BlogTalkRadio. She downloads it right into her iPod and listens to it on the go.

I co-host an Internet marketing show on BlogTalkRadio.com. Our show is on for thirty minutes every Saturday morning. We discuss all subjects related to Internet marketing and occasionally conduct an interview with a special guest on the show. You can find the show at www.blogtalkradio.com/beginnerinternetbiz. Setting up your own show is very simple. First, you sign up for an account and once you are a member you can start scheduling your own show. Since the shows on BlogTalkRadio are live, you have to schedule your show in advance.

You can make your show for as long as you want. The format works just like a real radio show. BlogTalkRadio gives you a guest number so callers can actually call into your show. There is also a chat feature so listeners can instant message questions or comments as well. You can even add bumper music at the beginning for an intro or create a commercial that you play during your show. If you're consistent in hosting these shows, you can build a huge following and maybe even get some big time sponsors. Once you've done your first show, BlogTalkRadio gives you the html code for a player to post on your blog or Web site so visitors to your site can listen to your show without logging onto BlogTalkRadio's site.

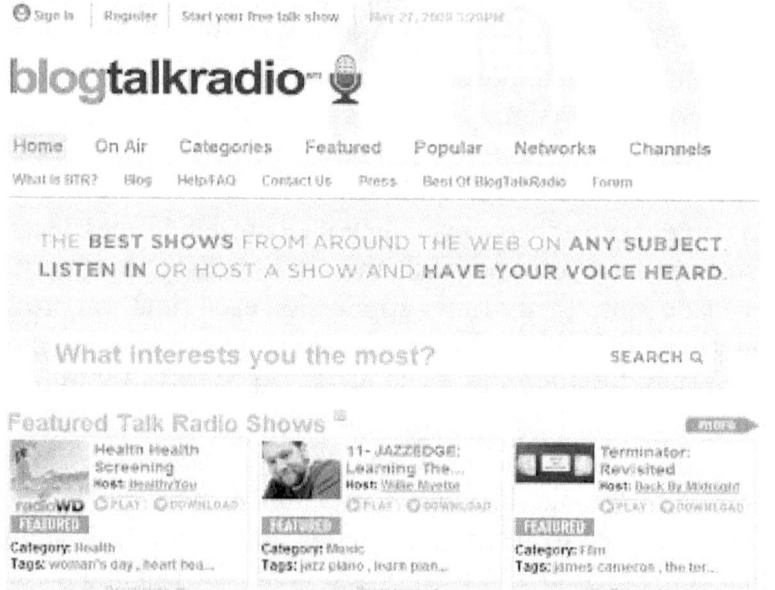

*Figure 3: BlogTalkRadio homepage.*

*Get two additional free gifts at: www.JonathanTaylorBlog.com/freegifts*

Podomatic.com is another Web site I've used for hosting my podcasts. The podcasts on this site are not recorded live. You can actually do the show whenever you want using a digital recorder, which is what I used in the early days of doing podcasts, or you can use a free software program called Audacity, a very simple sound recorder that allows you to edit audio files before you post them online.

### Adding "Juice" To Your Marketing

Podcasting is one of the best ways to add major search engine juice to your site. For each of the podcast shows that you create, you are allowed to enter keywords into that site. BlogTalkRadio allows you to add five keywords for each new show that you host. For my Internet marketing show, I usually choose keywords related to the topic of my show that are heavily searched for online.

Again, Google loves unique content. The more often you host a show, the more your rankings will climb. Use your podcast to promote your main Web site by talking about it at the end of your show or adding links to your posts. (You can also add blog posts along with your podcast.)

### Build a Subscriber List

Much like e-mail marketing, you want to build a following. With podcasting, you have the option of creating a free or paid for program, although it is highly unlikely people will pay to listen to podcasts these days with so much other free information. But the value in podcasting is building a listenership on iTunes or a fanbase on BlogTalkRadio who listen to your show each and every week. If you do this and provide good audio content, you can attract a large group of buyers who trust what you say.

### Developing Your Own Theme Show

If you're thinking of hosting your own show, use BlogTalk-Radio to host your live show and then take the audio file and upload it to your Podomatic account, as well. The more listeners, the better. As I mentioned, you can schedule your show times in advance, so if you are thinking of having a weekly show, make sure you try to stay consistent with the time and day of the week.

The more consistency you have, the more live listeners you're likely to gain. As I mentioned, I host an Internet marketing show every Saturday at 10:30 AM—same time, same channel. You can use your e-mail marketing campaign to send out reminders of your upcoming show each week. Let them know what the topic will be. By doing a weekly show over and over each week, you'll be seen as the go-to person in your industry.

Dan Miller, author of *48 Days to The Work You Love*, has a wonderful podcast each week on finding meaningful work that you love. I have listened to his show for about three years now. He does his show with nothing more than his computer, a headset, a sound mixer, and the free sound editing program, Audacity. His show has more than 120,000 downloads per month. I love podcasting because it's a simple way to get content out about your area of expertise. And once it's up, it stays up. I still get traffic from shows I've done two or three years ago!

Chapter Six

# Marketing with Social Networking Sites

While many hold the position that social networking sites are just another fad, other companies are embracing it and using it as a tool to build a stronger relationship with their customer base. Companies like Starbucks, Comcast, and Zappos are just a few of the many companies that are using social sites like Twitter and Facebook to present a more personal brand. They bring their companies to life by putting real voices behind the name. Zappos CEO Tony Hsieh adds his own casual personality by posting random "tweets" from time to time. Zappos employees even have their own Twitter accounts, which allow them to connect with loyal customers, providing them with updates and dealing with customer service problems directly.

If you ignore these new social networking sites as just another passing craze, you're missing out on some low-cost and effective ways to talk about your brand. I've already given you some examples of the effectiveness of blogging, video sharing, and podcasting. Now let's look at some social network sites that can benefit your company.

### MySpace

You can't talk about social media without mentioning MySpace, and quite frankly that's about all I'm going to do is mention them. Unless you're targeting a younger audience, I'd recommend spending time on other sites. The majority of the visitors to this site are under forty. Unless you're marketing something that appeals to teenagers, like video game action guides or your own rap album, look somewhere else. Personally, I consider my time valuable and if I'm going to spend time on social media sites, I want them to be with people who are similar in age and professional caliber.

That said, if you do have a product that you think would appeal to this mass audience, by all means, take your shot. Just make sure that you're able to speak the lingo of those in the twenty and younger audience or you'll look a little foolish.

Companies that are successful in launching MySpace marketing campaigns usually use fun promotions that invoke lots of interaction, competition, and bragging rights. Disney is a prime example of this. They don't just use MySpace to advertise a movie that's coming out. They spend time creating a MySpace site that allows users to participate in contests with a chance to appear in the movie or interact with the directors and stars.

**Facebook**

Facebook is one of the more popular social sites. What started out as a site for college students has expanded to people of all ages. I've spent more time than I should recently tracking down old high school buddies that I've lost contact with over the years. Facebook allows you to easily keep track of other people's activities, as well as sharing your own. While it can be a great marketing medium, you want to be careful not to promote too aggressively. People can get turned off if they see you taking advantage of a site that is meant to connect and build relationships. Instead, the best approach is a casual one that lets people in on what you're up to.

For example, my friend and professional fitness trainer, Kaleb White, shares what he's doing by uploading videos of his latest training tips with links to his Web site. Just recently he decided to launch a summer bootcamp. He had a new section added to his site that described the bootcamp. He then had a message posted that read

"Kaleb is preparing to launch his Summer Beach Body Bootcamp." The message was followed by a link to his site. Messages like this that simply let people know what you're involved with are more of a soft sell approach. And as the old saying goes "People like to buy, but they hate to be sold to."

Similarly, as I get closer to publishing this book, I'll be making updates as to where I am in the process. I'll probably post some links on my blog, add some video, and pictures of the first copy to come off the printing press. If you've got a new product launch, it's an easy way to share it with your network.

If I owned a landscaping business, I would use Facebook to keep my network up to date on my landscaping jobs. I'd also create a blog site that offered landscaping tips. I'd have the Web site listed on my profile page and post a link to the latest posts. I'd include pictures of recent work I had done for customers. I have another friend who is a self-employed handyman and remodeler who does excellent work. He occasionally posts pictures on Facebook of some of the latest jobs he's finished. It's a subtle way of promoting your business and it builds trust. People often do business with people they are familiar with.

### Do You Twitter?

Twitter is one of the fastest growing social media sites, so I'll spend a little more time discussing its business value. First, what is Twitter? Try to imagine a cross between blogging and texting to a large group. Twitter is really nothing more than a way to send short bursts of information to people who want to receive them. "Tweets," as they're known, are short messages consisting of no more than 140 characters. You can send these to others, as well as read updates from other people you might be following. Like Facebook, it's easy to search for people who are already using Twitter and once you find them, you can choose to follow them. In response, they'll likely respond by choosing to follow you. Thus, you begin building a network of people sending updates about what they're doing.

At this point, you're probably thinking that Twitter sounds like all the other social sites. This is true, but Twitter does offer some distinct advantages in the world of online marketing. One of the biggest advantages is that Twitter updates can work in conjunction with SMS text on your mobile phone. You don't have to have online access to post or read Tweets.

**Twitter for Business**

Twitter offers some great applications that can benefit your business. If you post a blog on a regular basis, you can use an application called Twitterfeed to automatically tweet your latest posts with links to your blog. This is a valuable tool especially if your blog is an integral part of your business. You can sign up for this tool at Twitterfeed.com. Once you sign in with your username and password, you just enter the url of the RSS feed. You can then specify how often you want Twitter to check for new content. Also, there is an option to include the blog title and description.

You can't upload pictures directly onto Twitter like Facebook or MySpace, but there are apps that allow you to link to and comment on photos. One application that I use for this is TwitPic. Just go to TwitPic.com, enter your username and password, then upload the photo, add comments, and you're done. This application comes in handy if you're someone that uses photos to describe your work. The best tweets are those that don't just tell what you're doing, but describe what you are doing. Remember, people are very visual, so send as many photos as you can of what you're currently working on. Occasionally, I like to take random pictures of people and interesting and strange things I come across while traveling. A picture is sometimes worth far more than a thousand words.

**Connecting with Your Customers**

Using Twitter to get customer feedback is another way of building trust. As I mentioned earlier, there are a number of companies that are using this strategy by having their employees set up Twitter accounts. Twitter can be used to get feedback on a new product launch or any changes that you are planning to make in regards to service.

Keep in mind that your followers only have 140 characters to post comments, so if you're looking for detailed comments, you might want them to e-mail you. Also, let your customers be honest with you. Brace yourself for whatever you get back. In doing so, the trust factor goes up. Not only that, but when they reply to your requests for comments, their followers see the reply as well, so you might end up getting a number of new follows and customers in the process.

Using Twitter as a means of customer support can be a real advantage. Companies like Starbucks, Jet Blue, Comcast, and Home Depot are just a few that are responding to complaints, answering questions, and posting troubleshooting tips.

 **comcastcares**

@lostprophyt Life is short, I'd look for the positives. There are so many things that can be negative, but life is really about much more

*3 minutes ago from web in reply to lostprophyt*

@fluidmarkup Not yet, still testing
*4 minutes ago from web in reply to fluidmarkup*

@lostprophyt I was not able to locate an account under your name to assist, but you know we are always here to help if you change your mind
*11 minutes ago from web in reply to lostprophyt*

@lostprophyt Is that our doing? Any company can but they have to run the wires with high cost.
*12 minutes ago from web in reply to lostprophyt*

*Figure 4: Comcast's Twitterfeed*

*Get two additional free gifts at: www.JonathanTaylorBlog.com/freegifts*

Want to find out what your followers might be saying about you or your company? An easy way is to use a service called Monitter (www.monitter.com). This service is a Twitter version of Google Alerts. It keeps track of certain keywords people are using when they post a tweet. By putting in your username or company name, you can keep track of what is being said about you in Twitterland.

### Twitter, the Virtual Office

We live in a day where communication is at the touch of button. With cell phones, texting, and instant messaging, anyone can maintain communication with the people they work with from just about any location. I've had freelancers do work for me in the past who I've never even met face to face. The only way I communicated with them was online through Yahoo Instant Messenger. If you've got a team of professionals that work for you, you know it's a lot easier to stay in touch via messenger or SMS texting, than making phone calls every time you need to inform them of something.

Twitter offers a feature that can keep your whole team on the same page at once. You can create a separate Twitter account just for your office team; you can keep in touch with everyone from any location. It's a great method for sales mangers to get updates from their sales team as a whole. In order to make sure your communication is secure and not being read by outsiders, just go to the settings page and click "protect my updates. " Then only people you approve will be allowed to see the posts.

### LinkedIn

LinkedIn is a social site specifically for business people who want to connect with other professionals. The site allows members to post their own resumes for everyone to see, as well as tap into the business contacts of others.

A person may only have twenty direct contacts when getting started, but that doesn't keep them from building their rolodex quickly by having indirect access to millions of other professionals on the site. If you're in the professional services of any type, this is a great way to meet potential clients. In order to build new contacts, you only need to request an introduction.

Premium members are able to use LinkedIn's mailing list manager service. LinkedIn also offers a feature called "Answers," where members can log into a forum and answer questions that others might have about specific topics. This is a great way to build your reputation as an industry expert. A CPA can quickly establish himself as the recognized expert by contributing answers to tax questions on a regular basis.

Members who offer answers are given scores based on the quality of their answers. In short, LinkedIn is a great resource for branding your own name, and finding others who can help your business. After all, business is about connecting with others.

**Meetup**

Meetup.com is another social networking site with a slightly different twist. Instead of networking with others online, the site is designed to help people organize groups in their area. In April of 2008, I organized my first small business marketing meetup in Knoxville,Tennessee. Our Knoxville meetup Web site is http://www.meetup.com/smallbiz-997/.

With no advertising on my part, the group has grown to eighty members. We meet once a month at a local computer learning center and discuss guerrilla marketing tactics. Each of the attending members, who are entrepreneurs themselves, is encouraged to share strategies that work in their industry. Meetup groups like this are happening all over the country for all sorts of interest groups.

Groups centered around robotics, hiking, books, parenting, knitting and crocheting, and movies are just a few of the many Meetup groups you'll find in my area. I also organize a second Meetup with a friend that helps teach Internet marketing. Becoming a member is completely free, however, small fees might be charged to attendees to cover the cost of meeting rooms and organizer's fees. There is a monthly fee for being an organizer, but it's less than twenty dollars a month.

Creating a Meetup group around your area of expertise is an effective way of positioning yourself as a recognized expert in your field. One of the members of our small business Meetup is a fitness coach and she has organized her own local health and fitness Meetup group. I could think of many other professions like CPA's, painters, landscapers, auto mechanics, web designers, and more who could benefit from building a local interest group, especially if you're new to an area and don't have many connections. Take time browsing all the interest groups at Meetup.com. It's sure to spark some ideas.

**Discussion Forums**

Online discussion forums are one of the best ways to find a hungry school of fish all in one place. Like other social media

*Figure 5: Knoxville's Small Business Marketing Meetup homepage*

*Get two additional free gifts at: www.JonathanTaylorBlog.com/freegifts*

sites, forums give you the opportunity to network, but in a specific niche. If you can become the expert offering advice to a group of people, they will click to your site. Just like other social network sites like LinkedIn, you have the opportunity to tout your knowledge base and answer questions that people may have. You can find forums for just about any topic by doing a simple Google search for the "key industry word + forum. " You can also use a site called www.big-boards.com.

If you are active long enough in a particular forum as a person that answers common questions, people will naturally visit your site for other information. This works out well, particularly if you are marketing information products online.

### Squidoo

Squidoo.com is another social media site that focuses more on a person's expertise or interest. Squidoo is a community of people who are building web pages, or "lenses. " Instead of networking, you're creating these Squidoo lenses that point readers to blogs, video, or other news content related to that particular niche.

You can use Squidoo to funnel people to your own Web site. For example, as I look at Squidoo, I can see a list of the top one hundred lenses for several different categories. If I were to click on the "Home & Garden" section, I would find that one of the top lenses is "Perfect Paint Colors for Your Home's Interior. " If I go to this lense, I find tips on picking the perfect paint color. I also find links to articles written by Kate Smith, the lense creator. She has a link to her site www.senationalcolor.com.

Squidoo lenses are a great way to build traffic through search engines. Currently, Google ranks lenses that are loaded with good content at higher importance. The key is content! Put as much information as possible on your Squidoo page. You have the option of adding videos, pictures, articles, surveys, and most important, links to your site! Squidoo pages are extremely easy to build. You can customize it using a series of modules, such as:

- YouTube—This site allows you to embed video on your lense. Google rewards your lense in the search engines the longer people stay on your page.
- Text Module—Each one of these allows 2,500 characters at a time.
- RSS Module—You can add the RSS feed from your main blog site if you already have one. Each time you update your blog, it posts to your Squidoo lense as well.
- Poll Module—This feature allows your visitors to interact with the site.

Remember, the key to building your lense is to use keywords just like you would in writing content for your blog. You may wonder why you should spend time building a Squidoo if you already have a blog. They are very similar, but my advice is to put as much content out there with links to your main site as possible. The goal in all of this is to build your brand. The Squidoo page should be funneling people to your blog or your main site.

While there seems to be an endless list of other social media sites out there, I'm not going to cover them all. Instead, I'm going to recommend ten more that might benefit your business by getting more exposure online.

1. http://en.wikipedia.org—The bigges feature of Wikipedia is being able to create your own business reference page. Outside of that you can use Wikipedia's Community Portal to connect with other professionals enthusiastic about news, business, research, and more.
2. http://www.wikihow.com—You can create how-to guides on this site which allows you to promote your company's services to the public for free.
3. http://www.ning.com—This site allows you to create your own social networking site. You can build free social networks around your particular niche or industry.

4. http://www.xing.com—A great business networking site that lets you network with specialized groups. XING is great for professionals who are interested in tapping into a network of contacts in other industries.

5. http://www.networkingforprofessionals.com—A community site that lets you post resumes, photos, video clips, articles you've written, and other parts of your online profile while you meet new business contacts.

6. http://www.ecademy.com—You can connect with other business people through the site's online blog and message-board chats, as well as its membership program, which awards exclusive benefits.

7. http://www.meetin.org—Similar to Meetup.com, but aimed at specifically making business connections in your city by networking through the site. This site lets members organize a local event.

8. http://www.buzzflash.net—This news site is great for contributing news articles on a variety of different subjects.

9. http://www.gather.com—social networking site for writers, authors, photographers, and bloggers. You can look at categories on money, books, health, and other news, news related to politics, business, and entertainment. Great tool for marketing research—finding out what certain segments of the public are talking about.

10. http://www.wetpaint.com—Allows you to create your own Wiki web page to promote your business.

# Chapter Seven

# Do Something!

I have only scratched the surface on most of the topics in this book. I could write an entire book about creating e-mail marketing campaigns or on building an effective blog site, but the point of this book is to make you aware of the direction marketing is taking. Radio Shack is using a great new slogan—"Don't just buy stuff, do stuff. " My conclusion is similar—"Don't just read about stuff, do stuff!"

Technologies may change, but the focus will still be the same—connect with customers and give lots of value. Different online services may come and go, but the fundamentals of building relationships with your customers will never change.

I suggest that you take these strategies and implement one or two at a time. Start with e-mail marketing. This is the one key strategy that you need to implement right away. Your company is wasting money every day if you don't have a system for capturing names and e-mail addresses when visitors come to your site.

Build a blog that provides solid content using video. Keep customers informed about the latest changes; offer solutions through tutorials. Take a lesson from Jim the realtor and Gary the wine expert. Host a weekly video show. Give good solid content that will keep people coming back again and again.

The point is to implement something. As I mentioned earlier, I host a local small business marketing meetup in Knoxville each month. We throw out a bunch of ideas during these two hour groups and at the end I find that many of the members are both excited and overwhelmed at the same time. Sometimes giving people too much information at one time isn't the best approach. Think back to my point in the book when we talked about the "Power of One" in terms of Web sites. As the saying goes, you eat an elephant one bite at a time. If you don't have the time to implement some of these online strategies, hire it out.

I've hired virtual assistants in the past who have done things for me like sending out cards, making business calls, adding articles to Web sites, posting articles on article directories, and more. You can hire a virtual assistant for very little cost. Most of them charge between $15-$20 and hour depending on their level of experience. You can usually buy blocks of time as well. I've purchased 10-12 hour blocks a week in the past. You'd be surprised how much they can accomplish for you in just ten hours a week.

This book is not meant to be complex. It's meant to give an overview of resources for branding you or your business online. I may get some criticism for not going into more step-by-step detail about how to use certain sites I've mentioned in this book, but my intent is simply to get the wheels turning so you can visit them yourself and find out if they can be a benefit for your business.

Following this are two bonus sections. One discusses an online tool that can be used very effectively for offline marketing. I have used it for the last two years in my business and would not include it in this book if I didn't think your business could grow substantially from using it.

The second is a transcript of a short interview I did with David Dutton, author of the book *Internet Empires.* In this short interview, I discuss with David his experience in the world of online marketing, and what he sees as the most crucial elements for trying to market your product or service online.

In interviewing David, and talking with clients and business associates each day, I've realized that the most crucial element for anyone is taking action on the ideas you learn.

Francis Bacon is credited with the phrase, "Knowledge is power," and many people still quote it today. But this phrase is only a half-truth. Knowledge only becomes powerful when it is applied. Now, go do something!

# Bonus Section One
# Using Online Greeting Cards

What we've talked about throughout this book is branding you or your business using online tools that most businesses fail to implement on a consistent basis. In this section, I want to share with you a powerful tool that assists in building long-term relationships with your clients and prospects. I will give you an intro into this system, since I already have a detailed report that you can download for free.

If you've been in business for any length of time, you understand the importance of getting a steady stream of qualified referrals. The problem with most professionals is that they don't have systems in place for getting a steady stream of qualified buyers.

There are three things that any business needs in order to generate a constant stream of referrals for their business.

1. You need a network of people that already know what you do;
2. You need to have established trust with this group; and
3. Most important, you need a system that can help you manage and keep up with your contacts.

You may be lacking in one of one of these already. For example, let's say you're just moving to a new region of the country and starting out in a fresh environment. You'll be lacking in the first two steps right out of the gate. But don't let this discourage you. You can overcome the first two easily if you have number three in place—a system to manage the network of relationships you're going to build.

But first let me share a story about a legendary sales professional. His name is Joe Girard.

According to the *Guinness Book of World Records,* Joe sold more automobiles for twelve consecutive years than any other salesman in the world! During his fifteen year sales career, Joe sold 13,001 new cars and trucks all at retail—no fleet wholesale or used vehicles! So what was Joe's secret to selling so many vehicles? Joe got referrals. Lots of them. In fact, all of Joe's business was based off of referral. Joe didn't hound customers who walked onto the car lot. Instead he had a system, a referral system that allowed him to stay in contact with his customers and prospects. Keep in mind, Joe was selling cars in the 1970s, so he had no computer based management system to keep up with his contacts.

Every contact Joe made, whether it be by phone or personal contact, he logged their information down into a card system he kept at his desk. He then sent each and every one of those contacts a unique greeting card every single month. In fact, as his list of contacts grew, Joe was eventually sending out nearly sixteen thousand hand written greeting cards per month! Can you imagine trying to send that many personal cards? Obviously he didn't do this all himself.

As I mentioned, Joe had a system. He hired two personal assistants who had the responsibility of sending out a personal greeting card to his list each month. This system generated so much success in his business that during the last twelve years of his career, he saw customers by appointment only!

Even with two personal assistants, sending out sixteen thousand cards can be difficult. Think of the work that's involved—they have to handwrite them, stuff them in envelopes, seal them, address them, and then send them out through the post office. With technology today, there is a much more efficient approach to sending out cards. One happens to be a system that I've used for the last two years.

I used to dread the holidays. Not for the reasons you might think. I dreaded them because I had to shop for cards and gifts for my best clients. I always wanted to give a personal touch, so I would normally handwrite and address all of those cards.

Then I discovered through a friend an amazing online system that lets you not only customize your own greeting cards, but also allows you to create card campaigns that can be managed right from your computer. For example, you can create a monthly greeting card or postcard campaign that is sent to your clients on a regular basis. Bob Burg, author of *Endless Referrals,* recommends sending out follow-up postcards to potential clients after the initial meeting. This helps to separate yourself from the pack. It generates top-of-mind positioning in the minds of your prospects.

Why did people buy cars from Joe Girard? Because Joe was the only car salesman sending them greeting cards every month and wishing them a holiday greeting for whatever the occasion was that month.

This online referral card system has more than eight thousand card templates to choose from. There's also a feature that let's you build your own cards by uploading digital pictures and creating captions and borders around them. I have amazed customers who've gotten greeting cards from me using this system.

This referral card system also has a contact management system so you can keep track of each contact and the cards you've sent them.

If you're interested in knowing more about this online tool, then go to my blog site www.jonathantaylorblog.com and download the free report, "The Referral Card Sales System: 5 Secrets for Getting More Sales in Any Economy" when you sign up for my newsletter. You'll get a PDF guide on how to create some incredible looking cards online that are mailed out to your customers or prospects.

# Bonus Section Two
## Interview with David Dutton

The following is a recent interview conducted with Internet marketing expert and author David Dutton on how small businesses can implement Internet marketing into their business to generate more customers and more revenue.

*Jonathan:* Today, I am on the phone with David Dutton. David is the author of the book *Internet Empires* and David has also published some other books and reports out there as well. He is known as the most connected man on the Internet and today we are going to be talking about online marketing and specifically we are going to talk a little bit about some search engine optimization and some other things like e-mail marketing and creating back links and things like that. Because I know a lot of people in the small business world, mainly in offline businesses aren't as familiar with it. So let's just jump right in. David thanks for joining me and thanks for doing the interview today.

*David:* Awesome. I love talking about this subject so thanks for having me.

*Jonathan:* Well David, the purpose of this interview, is part of a book that I am working on for creating online marketing for offline businesses. I know in your experience in dealing with a lot of small businesses, they tend to know little about internet marketing. I know I talked to a lot of small business owners who may have a web presence but when you start talking about search engine optimization, getting traffic to their site, they really don't have a strong understanding.

*David:* Right.

*Jonathan:* So I'd like to just talk a little bit about some specifics. I know that you have got a number of Web sites up right now, so let's just talk. As far as getting traffic to a Web site, what are some things that you see that people are missing out on? Mainly small business owners. I know you're mostly in the Internet marketing realm and I know this is second-hand stuff for someone like yourself but when you talk to entrepreneurs, what do you see that they are missing out on?

*David:* Sure. Well, you know, there is not just one thing that I think they are missing out on. And it's not necessarily their fault because as an entrepreneur you are juggling so many things.

*Jonathan:* Yeah.

*David:* Sometimes you are the accountant; sometimes you are the marketer.

*Jonathan:* Yes.

*David:* You are the business manager. You are the salesman. You are everything. You are a solo entrepreneur or just a really small business or whatever. So, you know, there are just a lot of things. There are so many hours in a day and all that.

*Jonathan:* Right.

*David:* But in saying that, the Internet is a big deal. The Internet can generate a lot of money even in a local small business. A lot of business owners neglect that. So what you want to look at is does it fit your overall strategy? I would say most entrepreneurs have a Web site, but is it doing anything? No. Most of them are not doing a thing.

*Jonathan:* Right.

*David:* That is sad because they could really be generating more revenue as I will give you some real world examples throughout this interview. The way I look at things, though, is it going to make you money. Okay? For instance, like when I buy at a book at Barnes and Nobles and it's $25. 00 and I'll read part of it in Barnes and Nobles and I ask myself, "Can I at least make $25. 00 off of this? Can I at least make $25. 00?" So if the answer is no then I will not buy the book.

*Jonathan:* Right.

*David:* Or whatever it is I am doing. You need to ask yourself, as a business owner, is "Can I make my web presence an asset and not a liability?"

*Jonathan:* Absolutely.

*David:* The answer is yes. It really is. Some people just don't know that.

*Jonathan:* Right. David, the one thing that I see is that people put up a Web site and they just think that having a Web site means people are going to come. And they may not even be that naive to think that once you get a Web site somebody is going to come. But some may actually think, "Okay, now I have got to get out and drum up some traffic to the site," but they do it the wrong way. They go out and spend all this money on radio advertising and— I am not downplaying radio by any means—but they are missing out on some key strategies online that could bring them some business, even locally.

*David:* Yeah, absolutely. Most of the stuff, I mean, you have got to understand, Jonathan, I have been doing this for about seven or eight years and I was broke when I started. I mean as broke as broke can get really. So I didn't have money to start all this stuff so a lot of it, I had to use free marketing methods. To this day, seven, eight years into this I still use free marketing methods, or almost free.

*Jonathan:* Yep.

*David:* A lot of them offer, I'd say at least 70 or 80 percent of them are free. For the local business owner, the majority like probably 80 or 90 percent are free. So, I try to teach people how to maximize that from Facebook to writing articles about your topic whether you are a Nashville Insurance agent or whatever your business is.

*Jonathan:* Let's specifically talk about some strategies like search engine optimization. Now, you know, most online marketers are pretty familiar with this and this is secondhand stuff but still you are dealing with people, a majority of people out there who are not online marketers, they are just small business owners so they don't know a whole lot about it. Break it down for me in layman's terms. Alright. What is search engine optimization because, in talking to small business owners about this stuff, it seems they just start to get this glazed overwhelmed look.

*David:* Right. Well, before I go into that I'd like to start out by saying that I am not, even though I am an Internet marketer and have been doing it for years; I am not the most technical guy in the world. That is not trying to be humble. That is just fact.

*Jonathan:* Yep.

*David:* I am more technical than most but, you know, there are so many more people who are more technical but the key is knowing people to go to. For instance, I had software installed for me today from a guy that lives in the United Kingdom for $10.

*Jonathan:* That's cheap.

*David:* Ten dollars. That guy did it. Now I even bought a $7. manual just to learn how to install it myself. Could I? Yeah, I could have done it.

*Jonathan:* Yeah.

*David:* But I got hung up on something, you know; one or two things. So I just said, "You know, I will just pay $10.00 and just have somebody do it while I am working on something else."

*Jonathan:* There you go.

*David:* The point is, don't let the technical stuff scare you. Just know what you need to accomplish and then work from there. You are a manager and that's what you want to look at yourself as, is a manager. So search engine optimization. I am going to paint you a picture instead of just giving you the technical stuff. Search engine optimization starts with the conversation that is happening in your prospects heads already. Okay? As we are doing this interview Jonathan there are people all across the world having conversations; some with themselves and some with another person involved. Some are talking about different dog breeds and some are talking about real estate in Puerto Rico

*Jonathan:* Yep.

*David:* Some are talking about juggling. Some are talking about movie reviews. I mean, it's just all these topics. Okay? — Some of those people are going to take that conversation to Google. About 65 percent of them will take that conversation and enter it into Google. They will type in keywords or phrases.

*Jonathan:* Yep.

*David:* Okay? Then what you want to do is optimize your site for those phrases, okay.

*Jonathan:* Yep.

*David:* So, whoever does it better is going to win. I am kind of simplifying this.

*Jonathan:* Right.

*David:* There are some things that you got to do but are not as hard as everyone thinks. So, let me give you a real world case study. One of my clients is a guy name Dave Rados; he's out of Murfreesboro, Tennessee. He heard me speak at one of my workshops; he said, "Yeah. I need a Web site. " I think he already had one actually but it was a liability and not an asset.

*Jonathan:* Yeah.

*David:* So my team created him one based on what I teach. And we made it for about $150.00; made a little WordPress blog. A real simple site; looked nice. And one thing we put on there were testimonials and case studies of what he had done for people. So he did that and I was done. I didn't even build the site, my team did it. I am an Internet marketer and I do web design but I don't do a lot of the web design. I have people who do it for me. So that's why I want you to have that mindset. Anyway, after I finished, he liked it, thought it was good, satisfied, "Thank you," "appreciate it. " Then, a few weeks later, I get an e-mail. Jonathan, I'll never forget this. It was on a Thursday about 9:00 in the morning. I got an e-mail from Dave Rados. It was a pretty long e-mail talking about how he got his first order from the Internet. A lady called him, set an appointment and he closed $2,200 in insurance that day.

*David:* So, that was 27 days after we built him a Web site. He turned $150.00 into $2,200.00.

*Jonathan:* And now that's a customer who obviously came to his site from certain keywords that you'd helped him with in optimizing his Web site.

*David:* Right. He is an insurance agent and he lives in Smyrna, Tennessee, so what we did, was optimized for phrases like Nashville Insurance, Nashville Insurance Agent, Smyrna Insurance, Smyrna Insurance Agent and all cities in the surrounding area so when people were typing that in, he'll pull up. And that's what he did. This lady typed in something like Nashville Insurance Agent or something similar, I don't know exactly what she typed in, but she typed in something like that and then went to this Web site and looked around, clicked on the testimonials, and he has tons of them because it's one of the biggest strategies I teach people to do. She looked at the testimonials and was blown away; called him up. He came to her work and closed $2,200.00 in insurance right there.

*Jonathan:* Wow.

*David:* And so all we did was enter the conversation that's happening in that lady's head.

*Jonathan:* Yep. And so, yeah, you took something as simple as using keywords. I know in my small business marketing meetup, we look at keywords. Sometimes we get together and search for certain types of business services like accounting, or real estate, or dental in a local geographical location. Most of the time, you're not going to have a heavy search volume but they are there.

*David:* Oh, absolutely. Yeah, you're totally not going to have a huge high demand. You know, maybe in real estate possibly. It just depends on your area but if you close one or two sales a week off of those twenty keyword searches then it certainly adds up.

*Jonathan:* Yeah, absolutely.

*David:* So that's how you want to look at it. You don't just rely just on the Internet, but, you know, we don't really have to worry about that because most people aren't utilizing it like they should, anyway.

*Jonathan:* Right.

*David:* I mean, if I was a home inspector or a plumber, a hair salon, massage therapist is another big one, it's a no-brainer. It's just a no-brainer.

*Jonathan:* Yep. Well, let's talk about content. You know, I see a lot of Web sites and they advertise, advertise, advertise—"We've been in business twenty years", "We have better quality." So many of them still use that brochure-type format, "Here's what we are. Here's what we do. "And they don't see the value or they neglect the value of content-providing information on their site. And I know with your experience, you do a lot of Web sites that are tailored to providing content.

*David:* Right, yeah, and it depends on your goal of what you're trying to do. Your main goal really should be to generate traffic . . .

*Jonathan:* Yep.

*David:* . . . and get that traffic to opt-in to your e-mail list. Okay, you want to build a list of a certain type of person, you know. People who need a roofing contractor in Knoxville, Tennessee, or people who are overweight or people that need a chiropractor . A certain type of person—when they go online, they're not looking to buy anything; they want an answer or solution to their problem. They want information.

*Jonathan:* Right.

*David:* So what you do is you write articles about what it is that you do. If you're a plumber, you optimize for Nashville Plumbing or Nashville Plumber. But what you do is you write articles on that site and give people tips. You could even do articles on how to do plumbing yourself if you wanted to. Now that sounds quite shocking, why would you want to do that? But here's a fact—most people have no desire to do their own plumbing. But because you're giving first, it shows that you know what you're talking about.

*David:* And you're probably a nice guy because you're giving, instead of trying to sell them. You're actually like, "Hey, let me try to help you. "

*Jonathan:* Absolutely. And it creates a little bit of value too. I mean if you're giving something, like some valuable information up front, you're giving people a reason to stay at your site just a little bit longer because people are reading your content online.

*David:* Yeah, absolutely. That's what people want. People buy by emotion but justify it by logic. And so they're looking emotionally, you know, for the solution to their problem, and then they're looking for logical reasons why they should call you.

*Jonathan:* Great Point.

*David:* You've got a picture—you've got pictures of you and your family, your site looks good. You're giving away a free ten-page report on the "5 Ways People Get Ripped off by Plumbers." Write a report, or create an audio CD that can be tailored to the conversations prospects are having in their head. They found you because they typed in Nashville Plumber.

*Jonathan:* So let's move on to something else. Another strategy is using links or back links in your site. I mean, that's something that I know that you do.

*David:* Sure. Well, here's the thing. This is April 2009, being the first day of April, I believe. And things change, okay? Things change in search engine optimization all the time. Right now, what works and—I'm not an authority on SEO, but I will tell you that just one of my sites alone gets five hundred visitors a day. And so that's just one and I have several, several Web sites. I've been doing this for years, so I will tell you right now, roughly about 90 percent of your success is back links; links to your Web site. And so—and not just links to your Web site. Let me give you an example; let me make sure I explain this correctly. Back links are links to your Web site on other people's Web sites. They're linking back to your Web site. They may say, "Hey, this site is really good, and here's the link to it."

*Jonathan:* Right.

*David:* Then you can write articles at the bottom, you know, put your name, John Smith is an expert at plumbing, and he does a report on "The 5 Ways to Avoid Getting Ripped off By a Plumber." When choosing a Nashville Plumber, call him or visit his site. Well, if you're trying to rank for Nashville Plumbing or Nashville Plumber, what you want to do is when you get links back to your site you want to make sure that the link says Nashville Plumbing like in the link, like in the click-able text.

*Jonathan:* So the clickable back links need to be keywords?

*David:* Exactly. And so the more you have of that, the more likely you're going to rank . . . right passed your competitors.

*Jonathan:* Right. Now there's different ways to get people to link back to your site. I know in the book I talked about several different ways you can get back links. But I know there are some tools also that you can use online to help you create a little better linking process, right?

*David:* Right, yeah. There are a lot of different things. I mean, you could create other sites from other blogs to link back to you. You know, maybe you post your articles on another site and have them link back to your site. You can go to Ezinearticles.com, which is really good. I use the service just as one of my tools; I use a service called 1waylinks.net. I could take an article and have it submitted to a thousand blogs if I wanted to.

*Jonathan:* I discuss using article directories in my book, but this 1waylinks.net sounds like a great way to build traffic as well

*David:* Yes. I can get several blogs all linking back to my Web site. So there are a lot of different strategies. I mean, you could link back to your Web site, you know, using YouTube. Maybe you do plumbing tips, you know, and then you link back to your Web site through your YouTube video, right?

*Jonathan:* Absolutely.

*David:* A lot of different ways.

*Jonathan:* Yeah, I think I mentioned in this book, a roofing company that I found just a while back online. They had all types of videos on roofing tips. If you had roofing leaks like I did a while back, and you had questions about what to do, This roofing company had all types of really cool informative videos onYouTube and they all linked back to their main site. So they're probably getting traffic from people in their geographical area that are coming to their site and saying, "Oh, look at this guy—you know, these guys are located down in my area and look at this information they give out, I need to call them."

*David:* Absolutely. And another thing that we're not even touching on because you were talking more really kind of about the technical side, but these YouTube videos give them the perceived expert status.

*Jonathan:* Yep.

*David:* It is a big deal because you know, when you write—if you write articles, if you publish articles or books or videos, or whatever it is, there is a perception in your prospect's mind that you're an expert. And then that defense goes down because you're not going to sell them plumbing. In fact, it's an honor for them to even do business with you because you are an expert.

*Jonathan:* Yeah.

*David:* And so that's how you want to—that's how you want to position yourself. I mean, I've already started getting leads. I posted some articles, this is just an example—I posted some articles last week and I posted another one this week and I'm already getting prospects from it because the content was so ridiculous, it was so awesome, that people were like, "Wow," and I went into a place where nobody knew who I was.

*David:* You know, they had a group of about three hundred people in this one group online. I wrote an article and then it was almost like instant expert status. And so people were like, "Oh, wow, I want to do business with him. "

*Jonathan:* Yeah.

*David:* And the same thing can happen locally. In fact, if you take some of the info that—Jonathan, I know that you're teaching in the book you really could dominate your market. It's like the Wild, Wild West still, even in 2009. Because most people won't take action.

*Jonathan:* That's right. Like you say, there are so many ways to generate back links and I know David that you write in some discussion forums online. There are so many different avenues that you can take depending on what your niche is. You can take part in discussion forums; there are article directories out there that you can post content on; there is Podcasting that you can use to get links and of course Video sites like YouTube. People see your name pop up in all these different outlets. And yeah, you become more of the expert online and people start to find you through all these links.

*David:* Oh, absolutely, absolutely.

*Jonathan:* Well, you—let's talk a little bit about e-mail marketing too because that's another aspect of marketing that I see a lot of businesses are not utilizing. I mean, it really baffles me in this day and age; we're living in 2009 and we still have small businesses that don't use e-mail marketing at all. They have a Web site up but I would say probably eighty percent of them still have no way of staying connected with a customer through e-mail.

*David:* That's hard to grasp.

*Jonathan:* Yeah.

*David:* Let me give you another example, I said I like case studies that actually teach people something in the real world, this is how it's done. Every now and then, I'll teach a local workshop on how to do Internet marketing. I do it through Meetup.com. And I built a list very, very, small: 54 people. I didn't even really do it, just to be honest with you. Meetup.com is a great service; it's free to join and basically they market the Web site for me. And so 54 people— I'd not even e-mailed them in almost a year. I did these workshops just as a hobby. But anyway I decided to do a workshop and this is about two weeks ago, and had the workshop, charged $60.00 and I limited it to ten people. And within two days after sending out four e-mails,

I generated $600.00. Now that's not a lot, but at the same time I literally created $600.00 from sending out a few e-mails. I just sent out e-mails.

*Jonathan:* Yeah.

*David:* That's the power of e-mail because these people joined a group called David Dutton's Internet Marketing Workshop. And I know all of those people wanted to generate more business online. So if you send the right offer to the right list at the right time, you're going to make money.

*Jonathan:* Yeah. And there's something very cool about that, David. What you just described, is a group that once they opted in to your e-mail list, they stay on your list. Some of these could lay dormant for a period of time but, you know, you go in there with a new campaign; a new offer look what you've done. You just generated new business from that. But if you have no way of capturing their e-mail address, then that's just lost revenue. It's much easier to sell to someone who's already done business with you.

*David:* Yeah, absolutely. And your existing customers are six times more likely to buy from you again if you keep in touch with them. So if you start a little e-mail newsletter and stay in touch with them once every thirty days, that's good. Also, your next referral is probably going to come from somebody who has already done business with you.

*Jonathan:* Yep.

*David:* So the more times that you contact them, the more likely you're going to get referrals. And through e-mail, you could go write four articles and go set it up in an e-mail campaign using AWeber.com, and you set it up and you— you can actually have it set to go out automatically. So when somebody subscribes, they get these four articles, maybe one a week for four weeks, and it's all on auto-pilot. But they don't know that because they it'll say, "Hi, Jonathan," "Hi, Bob. " It's all personalized.

*Jonathan:* Absolutely

*David:* And so that's just one way you can build good will and cross-sell.

*Jonathan:* It's a great way to create top of mind marketing. The more your name is in front of people, the more they think of you, you know.

*David:* Yeah.

*Jonathan:* It's like that in any relationship. It takes time to build and the more they see your name the more they recognize you.

*David:* Absolutely. We buy from people we know, like, and trust and the more they see you, the more they're going to get to know you and trust you and then they buy from you. So yeah, that's what you want to keep and realize when you build a list. I challenged my local business owners to build a list of 100 people. Now that sounds like a ton of people, but it's really not if you do it right, you know?

*Jonathan:* Yeah.

*David:* Offer something of value. You know, you could do joint ventures with other people that have lists, locally.

*Jonathan:* That's a great idea for local businesses.

*David:* Yeah, for your buddy that has an e-mail list that is a real estate agent, say, "Hey, would you mind letting your real estate prospecting clients know about my free plumbing report? And I'll do the same thing about with you by real estate. " So you might add another twenty people to your list just getting your buddy to mail out.

*Jonathan:* And those twenty people will be great prospects, since you've been recommended by someone they already trust.

*David:* Yeah, there are different ways to really get creative. If you build an e-mail list of a hundred people, you could do wonders and that's just so small, but locally you could do very well.

*Jonathan:* Now you mentioned using AWeber; that's one of the services that you use. I know there are a number of them out there. I use AWeber.com also. There's also ConstantContact.com and I don't know if you still use their service but I hear a lot of people talking about it. There is a slight difference between the two though.

*David:* Right, me personally, I've been an AWeber customer for about three years now. Does that tell you anything and I would not cancel it. In fact, if I started right now and I was broke, the very first thing that I would buy would be an AWeber account for $19 a month.

*Jonathan:* Yep, one of the best investments you can make.

*David:* And so that's the big thing. I used to promote Constant Contact; I think it's a great program, it's definitely in the top three or four but the only thing is at least as of this recording 2009, they do not have auto-responders. That's an important feature because you can set up e-mail auto-responders to go out automatically. I mean I have an e-mail list on whoisdaviddutton.com that has fourteen pre-written e-mails that start going out once someone signs up. And they go out once a week for 14 weeks. And so, all these people are still getting articles from me even as I'm doing an interview right now.

*Jonathan:* Right. And the other difference is that Constant Contact has an option for both single opt-in or double opt-in.

*David:* Right, and that's actually the reason why I like Constant Contact. That's why I keep promoting Constant Contact to local business owners because if you go to the Chamber of Commerce and you say, "Hey, Jonathan, I have this free report" and we hit it off and "I've got this free report on three ways you could do your plumbing yourself," or "Three ways people could get ripped off " or whatever it is, "I'd like to send it to you, could I get your name and e-mail address?"

*Jonathan:* Great Point.

*David:* Okay and then I can literally login to my account and just add you to the list. And so that's why I like that because that's what a lot of local business owners do. They're going to, you know, Chamber events and business after hours and luncheons and networking events and all that and so you can do that. Then you could also just say, "Hey, can I get your e-mail address and

I'll send you the link to my Web site" and tell them to opt-in themselves.

*Jonathan:* So for a local business, Constant Contact is a huge benefit.

*David:* Or however you want to do it. Both works but that's why I like Constant Contact locally. I was shocked that they didn't have an auto-responder. When someone subscribes through AWeber, there's an e-mail that is sent out immediately that says, "Hey listen, I can't send you e-mails until you confirm the link. "

*Jonathan:* It's sending out a message to the recipient that's verifying that they were the ones who requested to be one the list. Cuts down on spam complaints.

*David:* Which is a good thing is you have an international business because some people can be jerks. And they'll say you're spamming them, when they are the ones that opted-in because they have all this tracking to show what time they opt-in, their IP address; basically almost like their mailing address on their computer, the date. It has all that. So if they hit confirm, there is no denying it. Like they have no case in court.

*Jonathan:* Right. Yeah, it's kind of a good thing and a bad thing in a way. You're right; you do have to click the confirm link that is sent, but it probably takes away any claim of spam.

*David:* It's there to protect both parties. But you know— both services are good, I was just really disappointed when I went looking one day for myself for the auto-responder feature and they didn't have one but I've heard they were going to be adding it. Other than that, they're a great service.

*Jonathan:* So how often do you send out e-mails to your list?

*David:* Well, it depends. I like to send them out about once a week. There are all kinds of different ways you could do it. I've got people that write e-mails everyday, you know. I've got friends of mine that are in the business and they literally send out e-mails three times a day, not just to sell but also provide good content. And then they might sell something like in the PS or whatever. So

I try to do it once a week and I don't really have a certain day. To be honest with you, I just do it. And the way I e-mail; I e-mail you just like we're friends even though it's going out to thousands of people. I e-mail people like they are one person on my list.

I don't think that I have over 2,000 people; I think, you know, all I think about is like just that one person reading the e-mail.

*Jonathan:* Yeah, your e-mails have that personal touch. They read like you're having a conversation with me.

*David:* Yeah. I'll talk to one person at a time. Perception is reality and you want to be perceived as an expert and a giving person. You don't want to be perceived as somebody that is just selling something every time he e-mails his list. You don't want to be that guy.

*Jonathan:* No, you'll get people unsubscribing quick like that.

*David:* And the way you can avoid that is to give content first and then sell. So my strategy—I try to send maybe three e-mails of content; really good content, and then I'll sell something. Three e-mails of content and sell something. You could go, content, sell, content, and sell, if you wanted to. That's fine as well. That's how it works. But so people know okay, you know, this is going to make a great article or David's selling something. And so when you do sell something they take it more seriously.

*Jonathan:* That's a great strategy providing, you give excellent content first. Balance the sales offer by providing something of value to them; something free of charge. Because, you know, people like the free stuff. So if you're a company that installs home security alarms, you could send out an e-mail each week that offers tips on keeping your home more secure, or your neighborhood safer. Then you might follow that up with an e-mail that talks about your specials running on a new home security system.

*David:* Yeah, absolutely. And, you know, you're not a non-profit. That's the thing. You want to do this not only to build a relationship, but to make money. Now another thing you can do is give content every time but in the **PS** you sell something.

*Jonathan:* Yeah, good strategy.

*David:* I use that a lot. If you write good e-mails it works great. My e-mails are really short and to the point, but very conversational.

*Jonathan:* Absolutely.

*David:* Because my goal is to get people to hit the reply button and talk to me. Yeah, every time I write an e-mail, I want people to hit the reply button and talk to me so I can dialogue and build relationships. Then, the next time, they are thinking, "Oh yeah, I had an e-mail conversation or had a phone call with that guy. " And they open my e-mails more.

*Jonathan:* Yeah, I know you like to talk. You also like to tell stories occasionally. People love to read stories. Copywriters like to use stories to capture a prospect's attention. They'll use case studies like you mentioned earlier to talk about people who have personally benefitted from the product they are selling. People are just drawn in by drama, in general.

*David:* Yeah, absolutely. You definitely don't want to be boring.

*Jonathan:* Yeah, you want to keep the reader's attention. I've seen a lot of your e-mails that I've gotten and you've told stories of simple things that have happened, whether it's a tree getting blown through the windshield of your car or anything else that just happens out of the blue.

*David:* Right, yeah. I took a picture . . . just snapped a picture of it and got it to my e-mail list and just said, "Hey, here's what happened to me today. "

*Jonathan:* It's fascinating stuff. It just kind of draws you in because people are attracted to stories. That's why people like movies. I think it's why some people love to read other people's blogs. People love to read about the lives of others. You've got to capture their attention with something interesting, because people are bombarded with way too much junk these days.

*David:* Absolutely, once you lose the real estate in their

mind, you're done.

*Jonathan:* Yeah, I agree. That's a good way to put it.

*David:* You've got to have a place in their mind. It's called positioning, like Jack Troutman talks about it. You want to have a place in their mind because once that is gone then they realize that you're not really giving value; you're just kind of annoying; then you're done.

*Jonathan:* Yeah.

*David:* Just hang it up.

*Jonathan:* All right. Well let's just get one last thing and we're going to wrap it up. Let's play the hypothetical for a moment, David. Let's say I am a carpet cleaner who has been in the business. I have a Web site but it's nothing more than a brochure site—nothing but contact information. What are some of the first things that I should be thinking about in getting started? If you would, just summarize what we've talked about, but give me the first place to start.

*David:* What I would do is tell you exactly what I'm telling one of my other clients to do who is in the Aloe Vera niche and actually has more of an offline business. I would tell you to start gathering the e-mail addresses of your current customers. In his case, I asked him, "How many salesmen do you have?" He said, "I've got two. " I said "Okay, When they're not very busy selling, I want you to call them up, and tell them to call up all your current customers and get their e-mail address." After they gather all these customer e-mail addresses, you just add them to a list. When you call up these customers, you say, "Hey Mr. Customer, I just wrote this free report on how to get wine stains out of your carpet in one easy step. "

*Jonathan:* Okay . . . . great.

*David:* And then you ask them if you can send that report to them. Then get their e-mail address. That's what I would do first and then what I would do next is definitely get a good Web site up. It doesn't have to be fancy. It could be a WordPress blog, which is really good. I mean you'll need a domain and hosting and you'll have about $20.00 in it. Now that's really basic. Really for $20.00 total. You go get hosting for $10 a month and a $10.00 domain. You're good; you're technically in business. But you want to do a little bit more and make it look great. And so then you get an AWeber account setup and so you can build the e-mail list and then just start sending them offers. Content and then offers; and then ask them for referrals. And then over time, you sell more to your list just because you're keeping in touch with them. You can also monetize your intellectual property. People are typing in "carpet cleaning" in search engines so maybe you write a little eBook on carpet cleaning, on do-it-yourself carpet cleaning and then you sell the eBook for $20.00 or $30.00. And then you go from there. So, you know, that would be how I would tell somebody to get started right now.

*Jonathan:* What about social media sites. Do you recommend those for small businesses?

*David:* Yeah, I do. I don't play around on them as much as I should but I know there are sites like Twitter and Facebook. I like sites like Facebook, and Linked In; and the reason why I really like them is because they have tons and tons of traffic, people hangout there. For instance, I have four hundred friends on Facebook. And I wrote an article about internet marketing and making money online today and posted a link to it on Facebook. That article went out to four hundred people just like that. And so if you have a local business, you probably see your customers when you visit the grocery store or go out to a restaurant or when you go to church. Social Media sites help to bring you and your customers closer together. They get to see your personal side, which is great for building trust.

*Jonathan:* Oh, absolutely.

*David:* And people do hangout there. I believe that you go where everybody's at. Go where everybody's at and just add value, that's it. I wanted to attract some new prospects recently, so I went into a discussion forum that has about three hundred members. I have no idea how many of these people are active, but three hundred members; and instead of just saying "Hey, buy something from me," I just wrote a killer article that I knew would benefit so many of them.

*Jonathan:* You brought value and separated yourself as an expert.

*David:* Yeah. And so, I might not get a phone call or e-mail from somebody for like six months but at least they know, that this guy knows what he's doing. See, you go in there and write about Nashville Plumbing or carpet cleaning, Nashville Carpet Cleaner, you know, reveal sixteen mistakes people make then, you see that's powerful. People are convinced, "Oh, man, I need to call him up. "

*Jonathan:* So, what you're saying is instead of going in there and saying, "Hey, here's what I do and here's my Web site," you're saying to you join the discussion and be a solution to the problem and offer something of value upfront and, you know, you may not be getting business right away but it's going to come back eventually. And an important thing to realize is when you post an article with a link back to your site, that article stays up for a long time. Just in discussion forums alone, you can be generating traffic from articles for years.

*David:* Absolutely, and I will. And that's the cool thing about all this. The Internet lets you leave footprints.

*Jonathan:* Absolutely

*David:* So, anything you do people can track, so you've got to be careful too with what you do, but, you know, you leave good footprints and people will find you and your phone will ring and then out of this they'll call and you'll get more business. And again, just about everything that I said is completely free

*Jonathan:* That's right! You don't have to spend a lot of money to implement this. I mean, like you said, you can get started with a WordPress blog template, which is completely free, all you've got to do is pay for the hosting, get a domain and like you said, $20 and you're up. There are hundreds of free WordPress templates you can chose from for your site. You don't need to hire some web designer. Then just start providing some content on your blog and people will find you.

*David:* Oh yeah, absolutely. That's it. You just go in and add value and if you keep that in mind, then money will come and like you said, from the beginning, you've got to start out with a goal, what you want to do, and what you want your business to look like.

*Jonathan:* So true.

*David:* And as far as your online presence, you want to turn into an asset, not a liability. I don't care what business that you are in, if you're a local massage therapist, you could really separate yourself from the competition by using these strategies. The sad thing is, most of them don't, at least not in my neck of the woods. They don't have a clue. There's nobody who is really dominating the market here, but they could if they just did what we're talking about, and stayed consistent with it.

*Jonathan:* Well, David, I appreciate the time and it's been great. Thanks for the info. You have got a number of Web sites out. Tell me what the latest project is you're working on now.

*David:* Okay, well I have several sites but I'll give you two of them. One of them is closebiggerdeals.com. It features over twenty-eight detailed joint venture strategies and techniques for internet marketers that they can profit from right away. I talk about how I brokered an 8 million dollar deal when I was twenty three over a nine minute phone call; plus how I became a published author at age twenty-eight. I thought that people already knew how to connect with people like I do, but they really don't, so I just thought I'd come out with a course and I teach that— "See How I Became the Most Connected Man on the Internet." And then also if you want to learn how to make money online, you should go to whoisdaviddutton.com or you can type in *most connected man* in Google and you can find me as well and that site teaches you the different ways to generate money online.

*Jonathan:* And if you just type in most connected man,

David Dutton's name will pop up there at the top of the list on Google.

*David:* Absolutely, and that's a good example of search engine optimization.

*Jonathan:* A great way to brand yourself too. I mean, that's brilliant.

*David:* Well, thank you so much for the interview. I really enjoyed it and the last thing I want to leave the people listening to this or reading this is to simply take action, okay. This stuff actually works. I'm telling you from personal experience that it works. Now just go and do likewise.

*Jonathan:* Thanks a lot, David.

*David:* Bye, bye.

# Bibliography

1 Seth Godin, *Purple Cow: Transform Your Business by Being Remarkable* (New York: Portfolio, 2003).

2 Elsom Eldridge Jr. and Mark L. Eldridge, *How to Position Yourself as the Obvious Expert: Turbocharge Your Consulting or Coaching Business Now* (West Palm Beach, Fl: MasterMind Pub., 2004).

3 David Dutton, *Internet Empires.*

4 Bruce Horovitz, "Two 'Nobodies from Nowhere' Craft Winning Super Bowl Ad," *USA Today,* February 4, 2009.

5 Seth Godin, *Permission Marketing: Turning Strangers into Friends, and Friends into Customers* (New York: Simon & Schuster, 1999).

6 Jay Conrad Levinson, *Guerrilla Marketing: Secrets for Making Big Profits from Your Small Business* (Boston: Houghton Mifflin, 1984).

7 Claude C. Hopkins, *Scientific Advertising* (Chicago, 1923).

8 Elsom Eldridge Jr. and Mark L. Eldridge, *How to Position Yourself as the Obvious Expert: Turbocharge Your Consulting or Coaching Business Now* (West Palm Beach, Fl: MasterMind Pub., 2004).

9   Lisa Sabin-Wilson, *Wordpress for Dummies* (Indianapolis, In: Wiley Pub., Inc., 2008).

# Additional Resources

Alan Lastufka and Michael W. Dean, *YouTube: An Insider's Guide to Climbing the Charts* (O'Reilly Media, Inc., 2008).

Joel Comm, *Twitter Power: How to Dominate Your Market One Tweet at a Time* (Hoboken, NJ: John Wiley & Sons, Inc., 2009).

David Meerman Scott, *The New Rules of Marketing and P R: How to Use News Releases, Blogs, Podcasting, Viral Marketing, and Online Media to Reach Your Buyers Directly* (Hoboken, N. J. : John Wiley & Sons, Inc., 2007).

Paul Gillin, *Secrets of Social Media Marketing: How to Use Online Conversations and Customer Communities to Turbo-Charge Your Business* (Linden Publishing, 2008).

# Online Resources

- https://www.aweber.com—E-mail marketing software with auto-responder
- http://www.constantcontact.com—E-mail marketing software without auto-responder
- http://www.blogtalkradio.com—Create a free talk radio podcast
- http://www.podomatic.com—Another free podcast portal for sharing your audio content
- http://www.wordpress.org—Download the WordPress software to install on your server
- http://www.wordpress.org/extend/plugins—Plugins for WordPress blog
- http://www.wordpress.org/extend/themes—Download free WordPress templates
- http://www.wordpress.com—Free hosted WordPress blog
- http://www.technorati.com—A popular search engine for blogs
- http://www.youtube.com—Video sharing Web site
- http://www.tubemogul.com—Distr ibute your videos to multiple sites
- http://www.meetup.com—Organize groups in your community
- http://www.linkedin.com—Networking site for making business connections.
- http://www.twitter.com—A social messaging tool for staying connected in real time
- http://www.facebook.com—Social media tool for connecting with friends

- http://www.myspace.com—A popular social networking site where members have their own individual pages or "spaces"
- http://www.big-boards.com—A daily update of the largest message boards and forums on the web
- http://www.squidoo.com—A site for creating popular lenses for your niche
- http://www.traffikd.com/social-media-Web sites— complete categorical list of all social media and networking sites
- http://www.seoresearcher.com/files/article-dirs. txt— Listing of all article directories
- http://www.easypushbuttontraffic.com—software for content to multiple article and video directories at once
- http://www.elance.com—Great site for outsourcing programmers, designers, writers, and developers
- http://www.guru.com—Another site for outsourcing programmers, designers, writers, and developers
- http://www.rentacoder.com—Get custom software for your business developed

# Article Directories

- http://www.ezinearticles.com
- http://www.goarticles.com
- http://www.buzzle.com
- http://www.articlealley.com
- http://www.articledashboard.com
- http://www.webpronews.com
- http://www.articleclick.com
- http://www.amazines.com
- http://www.articlenexus.com/
- http://www.ideamarketers.com
- http://www.articlesphere.com

- http://www.articlesfactory.com
- http://www.article-buzz.com
- http://www.articledepot.net
- http://www.articlegarden.com
- http://www.articlecity.com
- http://www.articlesnatch.com
- http://www.upublish. info

# About the Author

Jonathan Taylor is the president of Brand-U Marketing, a consulting firm in Knoxville, Tennessee. Jonathan has worked with large corporations like Brunswick Inc. in helping to improve their marine manufacturing divisions, as well as small businesses seeking to implement better sales and marketing systems.

Jonathan is a veteran of the U. S Army and graduate of the University of Tennessee at Knoxville. He is the founder and organizer of the Knoxville Small Business Marketing Meetup. You can find more information on this meetup group by visiting www.meetup.com/smallbiz-997.

You can read his latest blog posts and subscribe to his newsletter at www.JonathanTaylorBlog.com.

www.ingramcontent.com/pod-product-compliance
Lightning Source LLC
Chambersburg PA
CBHW061146180526
45170CB00002B/642